HELP, I'M FAILING AS A MOM

HELP,
I'M FAILING
AS A MOM

*The Survival Guide to Raising
a Child with a Mood Disorder*

TANYA TREVETT

NEW YORK

LONDON • NASHVILLE • MELBOURNE • VANCOUVER

HELP, I'M FAILING AS A MOM
The Survival Guide to Raising a Child with a Mood Disorder

© 2021 TANYA TREVETT

Published in New York, New York, by Morgan James Publishing in partnership with Difference Press. Morgan James is a trademark of Morgan James, LLC. www.MorganJamesPublishing.com

ISBN 978-1-63195-039-1 paperback
ISBN 978-1-63195-040-7 eBook
ISBN 978-1-63195-041-4 audio
Library of Congress Control Number: 2020902183

Cover Design Concept:
Nakita Duncan

Cover Design:
Rachel Lopez
www.r2cdesign.com

Editor:
Emily Tuttle

Book Coaching:
The Author Incubator

Morgan James is a proud partner of Habitat for Humanity Peninsula and Greater Williamsburg. Partners in building since 2006.

Get involved today! Visit
www.MorganJamesBuilds.com

For Olivia, Ella, and Sienna, for having the courage and compassion to share our story with parents who are desperately seeking hope and healing within their own families.

TABLE OF CONTENTS

. . . .

CHAPTER 1

YOU'RE NOT ALONE
ON THIS JOURNEY

· ·

"Don't be afraid. I will sit with you in the dark and wait until the light comes"
— **Nadine Tomlinson**

Debbie's Story

Debbie is a forty-eight-year-old working mom and mother of two children: sixteen-year-old Sam and fourteen-year-old Alicia. When Sam was born, she left her job to become a stay-at-home mom. Then, when Alicia was four, she decided to go back to work at the ad agency she had left. Being a stay-at-home mom had its challenges, and she craved adult attention. Her husband, David, is an engineer who loves working long hours. To the outside world, they look like your typical middle-class family.

When Alicia was three, Debbie started wondering why she ever dreamed of becoming a mom. She was always very successful in her career in advertising, but she felt like a failure as a mom. Sam was bright, funny, polite, and well-behaved. Alicia, on the other hand, was a terror. She screamed, cried, and had tantrums for hours every day over the smallest things. Anything Debbie said to her would be met with a screeching, "No!" Alicia was explosive, physical, and wore Debbie down to the point where she doubted her ability to be an effective mother.

She often wondered how this could be her daughter. She reached out to her friends many times when Alicia was out of control, but they never offered any reasonable advice, as her daughter differed greatly from their children. They would share how they parented and shared names of books they read, but none of their suggestions ever helped Debbie with Alicia. In her eyes, her friends' children were perfect, like her son, Sam.

Most days, she felt like she was doing this thing called parenting alone. When David came home from work, the kids were usually asleep. He was cool and calm, passionate about golf and tennis, and always made time for himself. Debbie resented him for that, in a way. Debbie's life was her kids.

Debbie's kids are teens now and gone are the days of sit-down meals as a family. It is impossible with Alicia's anxiety and unpredictable moods. The smallest things set her off. If Debbie prepares the wrong meal, Alicia will rage. If Debbie gives her the wrong fork to use, she will explode with anger. More often than not, Alicia is not able to sit and eat without it triggering a tantrum. She also gets annoyed by sounds. If Sam is too loud or sings, she can't handle being in the same room and becomes explosive. Little things set her off quickly and with no warning.

Sam is in a nightly baseball league, and Alicia has therapy three times a week. When Debbie is not working, she is driving her kids to activities and appointments, all while running notoriously late. Their meals are not healthy, and it is beginning to show on her waist. Debbie used to work out every day before work, but now she is too tired to get up at 5:00 a.m. for the gym. Date nights and dining out with David are a thing of the past. Alicia is too old for sitters but is not capable of staying alone. Debbie's marriage is falling apart. She has no energy for David after a full day at work, then taking care of the kids, the animals, and the house. At the end of the day, she collapses, not knowing if she can do this all over again the next day.

Most days, David acts irritated. He is completely self-absorbed and unaware of the demands Debbie has as a full-time working mom with two children, one of whom has significant mental health needs. Alicia's needs are 24/7.

Some days, she attends school, but more often, she does not, because her anxiety causes her to avoid it. It paralyzes her. She is not able to get out of the car to cross the street or walk into a store to get food. She fears people will look at her. Everything she should be capable of doing at age fourteen, Debbie does for her. Debbie does it all.

They have tried every type of therapy and are currently in an outpatient program at a world-renowned hospital that is supposed to be the best. The problem is Alicia is treatment-resistant and her anxiety holds her back. Debbie's family is supportive, but they all say the obvious things, like "She needs more structure" and "Be firm." She knows how to parent a typical child. She knows how to use structure and be firm. She has a son who functions as a typical child and is doing exceptionally well at home and in school. He is on track to go to Harvard like his father.

Alicia is not typical. Her brain does not work the way Sam's brain works, and when Debbie tries to parent her the way she parents Sam, it is a disaster. Alicia is attached to her mother, but it is a love/hate relationship. Debbie never knows which Alicia she will get. One minute, Alicia is hugging Debbie saying, "I love you, Mommy" as though she is still two, and the next minute, she is screaming and swearing at her mother, calling her the unimaginable. Debbie walks on egg shells every minute of the day. Alicia has worn her down.

There are days Debbie no longer wants to be a mother. There are days she thinks she is failing as a mom and believes her kids deserve better. But she wakes up and does the routine again because she is a devoted mother and loves her children more than anything. Debbie is committed to giving them all that they need to be successful, happy, and healthy children so they can be successful and independent adults, but it is hard. She has no more energy.

Alicia first started therapy in preschool. They have switched therapists many times, as some have caused her behavior to get worse. They kept searching for help. Resources were not readily available and nobody talked about mental health. Debbie was never sure who to talk to about it. She was ashamed. Their insurance was also not good, and finding therapists who took their plan was challenging.

Alicia's grades started declining in fifth grade. That's also when she started avoiding school and lost most of her friends. She started hanging out with high-risk children and became a high risk herself. Debbie purchased every book imaginable. Her Kindle is currently loaded with six books on anxiety and mood disorders in children and teens. She never finished any of them. They all seem to say the same thing, and nothing has worked for her daughter. Debbie has also attended conferences at leading hospitals. Each time, she would walk away feeling inspired and hopeful, only to feel disappointed as the tips and resources shared never worked at home with Alicia. Or she would get home and forget how to implement them.

Alicia's days are filled with tantrums, uncertainty, anger, rage, and sadness. She has no purpose in life. She is failing all her classes, self-harming, and unable to maintain healthy relationships at home and school. It makes Debbie heartbroken to see Alicia's older brother so capable and successful, and Alicia unable to function. He gets embarrassed when his friends are over, as his sister is very unpredictable. She swears, hits, and kicks holes in walls in front of other kids and adults.

They never tell people Alicia has mental health issues. They told friends once, and those friends slowly drifted away. At a time Debbie needed them most, they vanished. Debbie and her family now hide in shame. Every time Alicia is suspended from school or caught drinking or smoking pot, her heart sinks and she tells herself, "I'm failing as a mom." Her blond-headed princess, who she gave birth to fourteen years ago, is not the girl she envisioned she would be.

What mother would predict their child would grow up and start using drugs in fifth grade? Debbie is a mother who values family, health, education, love, and success. Somehow, she failed to instill these values in her daughter. She wonders how she has failed Alicia so miserably. Will Alicia be able to live independently after high school? Will she even graduate high school? What Debbie desperately wants is for her daughter to understand that she is capable of creating a life worth living. Debbie wants Alicia to care about her life and future. Debbie is tired of power struggles and giving in. She is tired of doing all that Alicia should be capable of doing herself. Debbie wants to find a better way to parent Alicia so she can make goals and have a purpose in life. She wants to be proud of her daughter. Debbie wants to stop hiding and wants Alicia to stop running. She wants to smile again.

CHAPTER 2

SHE WON AGAIN

. . . .

"There is no greater agony than bearing an untold story inside of you."

– Maya Angelou

My Journal Entry—April 18, 2009

Screaming, nonstop laughing, running. Three very young daughters (five, three, one.) One weary mother. Trying to catch a plane. I chase them and finally grab a hold of them, stopping in my tracks. Collapsing next to my daughters, I pull them all close. The oldest pulls away and runs again. Down the long corridor. Screeching on top of her lungs, laughing hysterically. We will miss our flight. I raise my voice to stop her. I raise it louder. She runs faster, and I know she won't stop until I get her. I chase her with the other two following behind me, my baby screaming and my three-year-old laughing. My oldest daughter runs faster bumping into people and her screeching and laughing get louder. I finally catch her. I have tears in my eyes. She hits me over and over and pulls away from my grip. All eyes in the Atlanta airport on me. One mother. No control of her daughter. Help. I can't do this. My heart sinks. I am a failure. She won again.

My Journal Entry—August 20, 2018

Screaming, swearing, nonstop laughter. One mother. One fourteen-year-old daughter. Surrounded by four of her friends. Her friends nervously laugh and look at me with wide eyes as my daughter repeatedly swears at me, calling me the unimaginable. She talks quickly and loudly, unable to control herself. She starts making demands. I tell her no. With every no she hears, her anger grows. Full-blown tantrum. Rage. Her eyes like daggers. She threatens to hit me. She swears at me as loud as she can with fierce rage. Teenage hormones, combined with a diagnosis of disruptive mood dysregulation disorder (DMDD), ADHD, and anxiety. One mother, no control of her fourteen-year-

old daughter. Help. I can't do this. My heart aches. I am
a failure. She won again.

My Story

The day we finally received a diagnosis for our daughter
was strangely one of the happiest days of my life. For years and
years, I searched for the answer. Getting one was validation
that I wasn't losing my mind; she did, in fact, need help. It
also confirmed my suspicion that yes, she was different from
most of her peers. It was the sign I so desperately needed that
told me, maybe I wasn't the crappy mother I thought I was
after all. The diagnosis gave me confirmation that she was
a difficult child with serious mental health conditions that
required a different way of parenting.

Her diagnosis of a mood disorder was a blessing.
However, it did not take away the fact that she would still
live with the symptoms of her disorder.

The tantrums, rages, moodiness, irritability, anger,
unpredictable highs and lows, and difficulty calming down
were part of daily life with my daughter. I walked on egg
shells, day after day, minute after minute. What may have
looked like a normal family to the outside world was complete
chaos in our home. Nothing was normal. Ever. In fact, I
never used the word *normal* and always told my girls, "There
is no such thing as normal." Through the repeated chaos,
anger, sadness, and disbelief that this was our life, I held on

to hope that we would finally get the help she needed. With the right help, my child would finally function like a typical teen. Little did I know, it wouldn't be that easy.

After the diagnosis, came ER visit after ER visit, hospitalizations, an extended Community Based Acute Treatment stay, school suspensions, bullying, failure to attend school, and failing classes. Day after day, we lived in chaos. I left my teaching job to care for my teen daughter who was not able to manage in middle school. Each day was a battle. I received calls, texts, and pleas every day to come pick her up. She could barely function and neither could I.

Her younger sisters were impacted. My energy was devoted to my oldest daughter, leaving little left for my other two daughters. They suffered silently, listening to the tantrums and sometimes dealing with being the target of my oldest daughter's rages. They lived in fear, as did we all, never knowing what was coming next.

My marriage was also impacted. My husband couldn't fully grasp the amount of energy it took for me to care for my oldest daughter on a daily basis. She was so needy. I was always waiting for the next explosion, putting out fires, and waiting on her. When he arrived home from work, I wanted to hide in my room and escape the hell that was my day.

Her friends and extended family were impacted too. She had trouble maintaining healthy relationships. She pushed away those that loved her the most. She was silently suffering, embarrassed but afraid to admit it, so she hid from those who cared so deeply for her. Mental illness is ugly and touches too many.

Mental illness is confusing, even for those treating the patient, and even more confusing as a parent. So many symptoms overlap, making the true diagnosis unclear, and then there is the trial and error of finding the right medication and managing meds. And if that is not enough, there is the process of navigating the mental health system, which is supposed to be available to help people diagnosed with mental illness live lives that are fulfilling. What I have found is that there are not enough providers and services for the needs, making it virtually impossible to get the help you need, even with the best insurance. Paying out of pocket is astronomically expensive but sometimes the only option.

The stigma associated with mental illness prevents people with mental health conditions from fully integrating into their communities. This includes students with mental illness who have trouble integrating into school. Coming out of hospitalizations back into school, my daughter heard the most hurtful rumors, including her being sent to a mental hospital for trying to kill her family. There were rumors after rumors and friendships that were lost due to the stigma of mental illness. When one in five of our youth have a mental illness and virtually every person in our country knows someone who has a mental illness, or has one themselves, how can the stigma continue to be an issue in our country?

If you or your child has lost friends due to their mental illness or have endured hurtful rumors, you are not alone. Teachers, administrators, and staff are often not trained adequately to handle children with serious mental health conditions. It is not their fault, but because of this, it is the children who suffer. In many cases, mental illness is seen as a behavior issue and schools believe the child is in control. My daughter has been suspended and given detentions for "skipping classes" when she was seeking adult support to help manage her emotions. She has threatened to drop out of high school many times. I am deathly afraid that she will not graduate. When she was thirteen, she announced she would work at the local chain restaurant where servers are all young women flashing their well-endowed chests. I nearly died. She was serious. My child is crying out for help, and I am doing all I can as a mother to get her help, but it is not enough.

My daughter turned to drugs and cutting to self-medicate and self-soothe. Seeing cuts on her arms and legs was heart wrenching. Seeing her come into our home after being out with friends in the middle of the day completely stoned tore me apart. Every time she left my sight, I wondered if she would come back alive. Will this be the day she overdoses, gets raped, or gets arrested? These are all questions I have asked myself since my daughter was twelve.

Caring for my daughter with a mood disorder and comorbid illnesses has been the most difficult full-time job I have ever had. Day after day, I vow I will quit because

I can't possibly wake up and do this all over again. Most evenings end with my daughter telling me how much I suck at being a mom. Soon, she will be in high school, and I am amazed I am still her mom. She hasn't fired me and I haven't quit—nor will she nor I, for we are mother and daughter, with a bond like no other, a bond that is so dysfunctional to someone looking in from the outside, but one that we understand as mother and daughter. Mental illness is cruel, but as strange as it sounds, it can be loving and bring two souls together in the most beautiful way. It took me years to discover how to connect with my daughter and how to live with her in a healthier way. Fifteen years as a teacher, energy healer, and mother have led me to the WELLNESS process, a simple, eight-step process I created to help me live my life with energy, purpose, health, happiness, and love. It worked for me and many other moms, and now I am sharing it with you.

CHAPTER 3
HOW TO USE THE
WELLNESS PROCESS

. . . .

"Trust the process. We always end up right where we are
meant to be, right when we are meant to be there."

– Unknown

My Journal Entry—February 24, 2018

My heart is heavy. The pain is too deep to put into words. My daughter is in a psychiatric hospital. The fear I feel exceeds any fear I have ever felt. I am terrified. I am alone. How did I fail my daughter? I have attended seminars and workshops, read books and articles, and consulted with numerous doctors and therapists for years. I am exhausted. Here I am lying in my bed thinking about her in the hospital, which looks more like a jail. Why must we make people with mental illness feel like criminals? Is she sleeping yet? Is she terrified? Is she eating? Is she crying too? I am her mother. It is my responsibility to keep her safe and happy. My tears are flowing, and all too familiarly, I'm feeling like a failure with sadness flooding over every cell in my body. I can't keep living like this. There has to be a better way.

The WELLNESS Process

This book guides you through my WELLNESS process, eight simple steps to learn how to handle your child's mood disorder without feeling like you are failing as a mother. I intended for this book to be read from front to back as you are guided through the WELLNESS process. My eight-step process will teach you how to live with your child's mood disorder in a healthier way. My hope is that it will become your survival guide, and one that you will refer to during your daily struggles parenting your child.

Parenting a child with a mood disorder can be frightening, exhausting, and lonely. Maybe you have tried finding help from doctors and therapists, but nothing seems to work. You are left feeling overwhelmed, worried, and responsible for your child's mental illness. You often ask, "Why am I failing as a mother?" I, too, asked that question many times before

I found a healthier way to parent my daughter, who lives with a mood disorder and other comorbid mental illnesses. The healthier way was the WELLNESS process that I created to change my life. It takes time, patience, and trust, but the results are so worth it!

One thing I know for sure is that change is scary. If you are afraid of making a life change, you are not alone. This is common. We let fear stop us from making changes that can change our lives. One reason we do this is because we are more comfortable with what we know versus the unknown. We also make excuses. "I don't have time," or, "It won't work," or, "It's too hard." In this book, I am going to ask you to step out of your comfort zone and do things a little differently.

We are wired to think with fear and doubt ourselves. But what if I tell you that you have options and your current parenting situation does not have to be the way it is? Can you envision your life as a mom as joyful, successful, confident, and beautiful? It can be. Take five minutes to envision what you would like your role as a mom to look like. Write this information in your journal so you can refer back to it later. If you don't have a journal, please consider getting one, as it will help you immensely on this journey.

This book is filled with ideas, resources, and tools that I have used in my fifteen-year journey as a mom, special educator, mental health coach, and energy healer to help you learn the secret to letting go of the guilt, so you can be a healthier and happier parent. You will understand the complexities of mood disorders and why it takes a village to parent a child with mental health conditions. I will share methods and activities for hope and healing for both you and your child. You will learn how to reclaim your emotional health and your life. As you incorporate my simple eight-step WELLNESS process in your daily life, you will begin to rediscover the joy, pride, and unconditional love you have for your child. Trust the process and trust yourself.

The eight steps of the WELLNESS process are outlined below:

1. What's Wrong with My Child?
2. Eek! I Am Failing as a Mom!
3. Letting in Light
4. Let's Build a Toolbox
5. Negative Self-Talk Not Allowed
6. Every Little Thing Will Be OK!
7. Support Looks Like This
8. Shine On, Mama Bear—You Are Rocking This Role!

Now I am going to ask you to pause and breathe for a minute. Take a big breath in for a count of three, letting your belly expand, and then blow all the air out for a count of five. Repeat this three times. Excellent, now you are ready to read on!

The eight steps above might look daunting at first, but they are not. They are simple, and I will be with you to walk you through them. Here is a brief overview of what you can expect as we go through the WELLNESS process.

In step one of the WELLNESS process, "What's Wrong with My Child?" I will give you an overview of mood disorders, including symptoms and different types, the prevalence of mood disorders, and comorbid illnesses.

In step two, "Eek! I Am Failing as a Mom," I will address parenting typical kids versus kids with mental health challenges. I will also talk about roadblocks. They are inevitable and should be expected, but now, you will have a new way to handle them. Finally, I will discuss how and why you need to be a mama bear. You'll learn you are not alone and you are not failing.

In step three, "Letting in Light," I will discuss acceptance, mindfulness, ways to practice it at home, and the stages of grief. Do not let this freak you out. Breathe. I am so excited for you, as you are going to begin to let light shine in and your days will become brighter.

In step four, "Let's Build a Toolbox", we will do just that! Together, we will create a box of tools (a calming box) you or your child can use to regulate yourselves during emotional distress. You will finish this step armed with tools and resources to make you successful.

In step five, "Negative Self-Talk Not Allowed," you will learn how to love yourself and accept your child in a new way. It's scary, but remember, you are not alone. I will walk you through this step, and you will feel the stress melt away and the love for your child pour into your heart.

Next, in step six, "Every Little Thing Will Be OK!" I will teach you how to breathe the right way. I will share some of my favorite ways to practice self-care and some of my favorite mantras. You deserve this, and you need this. Don't let your ego convince you that you are not worthy of taking the time to care for yourself. Like you, I am a busy mom, with little free time. I'll show you how to take care of yourself without neglecting your other responsibilities.

In step seven, "Support Looks Like This," I will walk you through the simple steps of building a tribe or sisterhood. This will change your life. You will walk away knowing you are surrounded by love and support and you will realize that you will never walk this journey alone.

Lastly, step eight, "Shine on Mama Bear, You Are Rocking This Role," will be the final step in the WELLNESS process, where you will rediscover the mom that you were meant to be. You will learn simple exercises that will allow you to rock this role called "mother."

As with most things in life, the WELLNESS process takes time and patience. As a parent of a child with a mental illness, you most likely already know there are no quick fixes in life, and the same is true in your journey parenting a child with mental illnesses. I am here to tell you, however, that there are better and healthier ways to parent your child with a mood disorder. My WELLNESS process has helped my family and many others, and I am excited to introduce it to you! Let's get started!

CHAPTER 4

STEP 1—WHAT'S WRONG WITH MY CHILD?

. . . .

"It's an odd paradox that a society, which can now speak openly and unabashedly about topics that were once unspeakable, still remains largely silent when it comes to mental illness."

– Glenn Close

My Journal Entry—October 7, 2009

I knew motherhood wouldn't be all joy, sweet kisses, and endearing giggles, but I wasn't prepared for just what it would entail. Olivia hopped off the kindergarten school bus looking glum today. I asked how her day was, and she replied in her typical manner—screaming, hitting, and kicking. After school was always meltdown time for her, but today she was willing to share more. "At recess all I wanna do is lie on the ground alone and stare up at the sky," she screamed. She indicated an ongoing friendship issue and feeling alone. After two questions, she quickly became more annoyed and ran off. I am sitting on my bathroom floor, alone and confused. The past three years at home have been so challenging with Olivia. Tantrums, anger, and physical aggression far outweighed the giggles and joy that childhood and motherhood were supposed to bring. Who should I talk to? The teacher? A therapist? Her pediatrician? Is this just a phase? The pediatrician told me tantrums are "normal" and Olivia's probably just "overtired." Her preschool and kindergarten teachers said she is perfect and doing great in school. What is wrong with my child? This can't possibly be "normal."

Her First Therapist—November 2, 2009

Three weeks later, I am sitting in the waiting room at a pediatric therapist's office with my kindergartner wondering how and why this could be happening. The room is lined with chairs. There are games in one corner and a small table with coloring in another corner. Pictures of inspirational quotes line the walls. Is this supposed to make me feel better? We sit and wait. Olivia grows inpatient. Waiting is not her thing.

Am I overreacting? Does she really need help? Is she just going through a phase? This was just the beginning of our journey. I felt alone. I didn't have any other friends who had children with mental health problems, or so I thought, so I didn't share this with my friends, and carried on as though we were the picture-perfect suburban family, living the American dream.

Little did I know in 2009, that this would be the beginning of a nightmare. Years and years of doctor appointments, google searches, appointments with therapists, and searches for answers led to one roadblock after another. Approximately eight years later, we finally had a diagnosis. In fact, we had a handful of diagnoses.

Mood Disorders

What Are They?

Mood disorders are still thought to be one of the most underdiagnosed mental health illnesses among youth. This was not surprising to me, as it took years for me to finally get a doctor to diagnose my daughter. Although it is not well known what causes a mood disorder in youth, it is thought to be due to a chemical imbalance in the brain, which can occur alone or in combination with stress or life events (such as parents divorcing, a death in family, money problems in family, etc.) There can be a genetic link with mood disorders, but there isn't always. The term *mood disorder* is broad enough to include bipolar disorder, as well as types of depression. Mood disorders affect moods, which can range from depressed (low) to manic or irritable (high).

Most Common Mood Disorders
- Major depressive disorder (clinical depression)
- Bipolar disorder (I and II)
- Disruptive mood dysregulation disorder (DMDD)
- Persistent depressive disorder
- Substance-induced mood disorder
- Premenstrual dysmorphic disorder (PMDD)
- Mood disorder caused by a health problem (cancer, chronic illness)

Symptoms of Mood Disorders
- Low self-esteem
- Ongoing sadness
- Hopelessness
- Low energy
- Trouble with relationships
- Weight gain or loss
- Trouble focusing
- Suicidal thoughts or plans
- Sleep problems
- Irritability, anger

- Loss of interest in things once enjoyed
- Rebellious behavior
- Decline in school performance
- Increase in complaints of physical symptoms (headaches, stomachaches)

Mental illness is an epidemic not only in our country but also worldwide. A shocking one in six children ages two to eight (or 17 percent) have a diagnosed behavioral, developmental, or mental disorder in the United States.[1] It was even more alarming to me that 20 percent of youth ages thirteen to seventeen have or will have a serious mental health illness.[2] In the United States, 11 percent of youth have a mood disorder, 10 percent have a conduct or behavior disorder, and 8 percent have an anxiety disorder.[3] The impact mental illness has on our youth needs to be addressed as a crisis in our country. Schools are unable to handle the influx of students with mental illness, as they lack funding, training, and staff to handle the issues. Teachers also lack time and are unable to add a full mental health curriculum to their already busy days.

The stigma attached to a mental health diagnosis is shameful to children and families. We can no longer sit on the sidelines and pretend this will go away. A staggering 70 percent of youth in state juvenile justice systems have a

---

1   https://www.cdc.gov/childrensmentalhealth/data.html#ref
2   National Institute of Mental Health, www.nimh.nih.gov
3   National Institute of Mental Health, www.nimh.nih.gov

mental illness. Fifty percent of youth ages fourteen and older with a diagnosed mental health illness will drop out of high school. Sadly, suicide is the third cause of death in youth ten to twenty-four in our country and 90 percent of those children have an underlying mental illness.[4] Many children are not getting treatment they desperately need for many reasons; parents have difficulty navigating the mental health system, whether it be lack of insurance, lack of providers, lack of hospital beds, and the list goes on.

Prevalence of Mood Disorders in Teenage Girls

Why are teenage girls more at risk for mood disorders than boys? Up until puberty, the prevalence of mood disorders is the same in boys and girls. However, after puberty, girls are twice as likely to have a mood disorder or anxiety than boys. Through brain scans, doctors know that boys and girls process emotional stimuli differently. Girls are faster to mature than boys in regard to emotional recognition, which in turn can make them more susceptible to anxiety or depression.

As a parent, I had a difficult time trying to figure out what symptoms were caused by "normal" teenage hormones versus what was related to a mental health illness. Doctors, therapists, and friends were quick to say, "Oh, it is hormonal. This is normal." However, it was so much more than the typical irritable attitude of a hormonal teenage girl. She had all the signs and symptoms of depression and anxiety, but

---

4   National Institute of Mental Health, www.nimh.nih.gov

getting the doctors and teachers to listen was another story. She also had symptoms of ADHD, which I brought up to every teacher starting in kindergarten. But all were quick to dismiss it because she didn't present the way other students, especially boys, presented with ADHD. Typically, teachers see boys present the most noticeable symptoms of hyperactive-impulsive ADHD. But teachers are not looking for signs of inattentive ADHD, especially in elementary school.

Many times, those children go under the radar. When Olivia was unable to finish a task, I would be told by teachers it was due to her "perfectionism," not because of inattentiveness. Unfortunately, my gut was right, and the teachers were wrong. At the beginning of seventh grade, after extensive neuropsychology testing, Olivia was diagnosed with inattentive ADHD, and interestingly enough, the psychologist who tested her showed me teacher comments on all of her reports cards, starting in PreK, indicating she had attention issues. Lesson learned; follow your mama gut, as it is seldom wrong. You truly know your child better than anyone else.

Comorbid Illnesses That Can Occur with Mood Disorders

- Anxiety
- ADHD
- Eating disorders
- Substance Use

- Conduct disorders
- Self-Harm—Although this is not in itself a mental health illness, but rather a behavior, it is often associated with borderline personality disorder, PTSD, anxiety, depression and eating disorders. The action of self-harm, or purposely hurting oneself (for example, by cutting), indicates that the person does not have the coping skills to manage their emotions.[5]

Having a mood disorder alone is traumatic enough for the child and their family, but what happens when there is more than one illness or behavior that is impacting the health of the child? Comorbid illnesses, such as anxiety and depression, can be more challenging to treat. Accurate diagnoses can take longer and delay appropriate treatment. My daughter's diagnoses came approximately nine years after our first therapy visit. Nobody wanted to misdiagnosis or have her labeled. I didn't want her labeled either, but we needed a diagnosis for her treatment and my sanity. Getting the diagnoses were scary, but also a relief. Finally, we had our answer, the answer I had been searching for. I have learned that so many of these illnesses have overlapping symptoms. I understand how difficult it can be to diagnosis a child and know that diagnoses can change as the child continues to develop.

Now What?

---

5   Self-Harm NAMI

Now that you have this information, how will it help you on your journey? Knowledge is power. The more you know about your child's mood disorder and comorbid illnesses, the easier it will be to navigate the mental health system and your child's school. The more knowledgeable you are, the easier it will be communicating with providers. One thing I encourage is to keep a journal of symptoms, triggers, and specific incidents when your child had trouble self-regulating their emotions. What helped ground them? What triggered them more? This information will be helpful when you meet with new providers. You can do the same when your child is starting new medications. It is impossible to memorize everything, so keeping a journal or notebook with dates will only benefit your child. Your child's treatment team will have an easier time choosing treatment options with this information. I also hope you feel much less alone now that you know just how prevalent mental illness is in our country.

CHAPTER 5

STEP 2—EEK! I AM FAILING AS A MOM!

· ·

"I have endured pain and loss, I have felt broken, I have known hardship, and I have felt lost and alone. But here I stand, trying to move forward, one day at a time. I will remember the lessons in my life because they are making me who I am. Stronger."

— a warrior, HealthyPlace.com

My Journal Entry Monday, December 17, 2018

It's eight days before Christmas and one day before my youngest daughter's tenth birthday. It is supposed to be the most joyous time of the year. It's

8:24 a.m. and the texts from my oldest daughter start rolling in, one after another. She has been in school for exactly nineteen minutes. She's angry, very angry. She's lost. She needs help. She's sobbing. Losing control with each passing minute. The texts keep rolling in:

"Pick me up

Hurry up

Pick me up in front of the office

U have to help me

Help

I'm crying mom please

I actually need you

Answer me now

I can't do it

Come get me now

I'm going to be sick help

I feel so alone

You suck at being a mother

All you do is listen to "professionals" who tell you what to do

Well I can't do it anymore

I need my mother

And idk why it is so hard for you

I am crying in school and you won't help me

What is wrong with you

PLEASE HELP ME

I NEED HELP

PLEASE

I'm sobbing

I can't go to the office because I don't have permission to be there

I need you right now

This is why I truly don't appreciate or like you at all

I need your help because I have nowhere else to go

Please

Come get me

I CAN'T GO TO GUIDANCE SO PLEASE TALK TO ME

MOM HELP

I'M WALKING OUT OF SCHOOL

I'm done

I'm actually walking out

Help

I made a stupid decision

Plz

Come get me

I'm near the park"

8:38 am:

Fourteen minutes of unanswered texts because I was instructed by the school not to reply to Olivia's texts when she is at school. They told me they will help her in school. I ignored the texts and my daughter walked out of school, just like that. Nobody at school knows she is gone. My heart races, panic sets in. I am paralyzed with fear. Tears can't come. I'm numb.

I quickly email the school to let them know she left. I had been emailing her psychologist when the texts were rolling in, and I told her Olivia needed help. I was told Olivia would have to wait, as they were in a meeting. I know all too well that my daughter can't wait. She has multiple mental health illnesses. When she needs help, she needs it immediately. She gets frantic. She's demanding. She's controlling. She is impossible. I call school to let them know Olivia has left the building, and I am on my way to get her.

At the edge of the park I see her walking quickly. I pull over and she gets into my car. Tears streaming down her face. "I know I made a bad choice, Mom," she says through her tears. "I didn't know what else to do. I needed help, and you weren't there for me," she added. My heart sinks. My heart physically aches. Real heartache, chronic heartache, caused by my fourteen-year-old daughter's mental illnesses. This is what my heart feels like day in and out. Pain. Deep pain felt at the core of my being. There is not a single day I don't feel this pain at one point or another as mental illnesses do not take vacation days.

Parenting Typical Kids versus Kids with Mental Illness

Many moms reading my journal entry would offer support and advice, sincerely trying to help. The problem is moms who have typical children would not know how to parent children who have mood disorders, like mine or yours. I was raised to be kind, respectful, honest, caring, and trustworthy. My children have been raised with the same values my parents raised me with. Mental illness does not care about values. Mental illness is cruel and can make the best parent look like and feel like a failure.

My days as a mom are spent in fight or flight, twenty-four hours a day, seven days a week. No breaks and little joy. This is mental illness. It is ugly. It causes pain. It causes parents to feel like failures. There have been so many days I have driven down the highway, thinking if I just drove off the road right here, my pain would be gone, but what would that accomplish? Nothing. I would inflict lasting pain on my daughters and my family. My actions would also teach my children that there is no hope with mental illness. Each time I get to that very dark place, when I scream and sob and say, "I can't do it anymore," I remind myself that I can do it, I am doing it. I repeat over and over, "I can do it, I am doing it."

I have talked to enough moms who are raising kids with mental health issues to know that my days are not unique. My days are like the days of so many other moms who share this journey of parenting a child with a mood disorder. You are not alone and you are not failing. During those dark days or moments, remind yourself of that. When you hear yourself scream, "I can't do this anymore," remind yourself that you can do it, you are doing it. Condition yourself to say this every single time you feel yourself getting lost among the darkness. This simple exercise will help bring you from darkness into the light.

There will be roadblocks, so be physically and mentally prepared for them. You will learn how to handle challenges more effectively and you won't let them stop you. But how? First, let's talk about your emotional health and what might be impacting your emotional well-being. As you go through your day, keep your journal handy and keep track of things that are positively and negatively influencing your emotional state. For me, on the top of my list for negatively impacting me was my social media use. After journaling for two weeks, I noticed social media was bringing me down and causing some unnecessary road blocks. Does social media do the same to you? Do you find yourself comparing yourself or your child to others who post on social media?

Social media is meant to increase connectivity. When I looked back at my journal, I saw that the connections I had on social media were negatively impacting me. Look at your connections. Are they healthy? Are they bringing you down? Are you really portraying who you are, who your kids are? Or are you, like so many others, posting what you wish your life looked like? If you are posting what you wish your life was like, you are not living an authentic life and you are hiding from reality. Think about how you feel when you are trying to portray someone you are not.

After my breast cancer diagnosis, I took a two-year hiatus from one popular site. The site provided me much-needed support during my cancer battle, and I was grateful for my friends. As I was fighting cancer, my daughter was fighting the demons of mental illness. It was the most terrifying time as a mother, as I watched my daughter drift away from her friends and school. As soon as I was well enough, my undivided attention went to help her cope and get the support she needed.

During this time, social media was beginning to drag me down. No longer did I find it supportive. I noticed moms posting the most beautiful pictures of their kids, all immaculately dressed, holding awards and certificates, and boasting about their accomplishments. Part of me felt happy for them and their children, but a larger part of me felt immense sadness that my daughter was no longer like these children. She used to hold certificates, win awards, play soccer, read books, enjoy writing, but slowly she lost interest in everything. Not only could I not take pictures of her because she was unwilling, but I had nothing to share with my friends on social media. What would I even post? Our days were filled with sadness, fear, anger, and hopelessness.

Compared to the moms I followed on social media, I felt like a huge failure. The sadness I felt at watching my daughter spiral out of control from her mental illness was unbearable. I needed time to accept my daughter for who she was and stop comparing her to other girls, so I took a break from social media. I eventually found my way back, as I connected to women in private support groups. I found this to be uplifting and supportive. More about this later, but for now, if you are finding that social media posts are bringing you down, rather than lifting you up, take a break and when you are ready to come back, you will have a new outlook on social media.

Release Your Inner Mama Bear

Don't let the challenges of raising a child with a mood disorder get you down. Challenges are inevitable. Expect them and you will learn to accept them and find a way to overcome them. We all know the term mama bear. I was the type of mom who silently and respectfully fought for my children. I noticed that I would walk away from school meetings or doctor appointments feeling defeated, as I never spoke up when school staff or doctors said something that was not true. I allowed them to say it. I would walk away and beat myself up. After a year, I decided I had enough. It was time to turn into a mama bear.

Have you ever come face to face with a bear in the woods? I haven't either, but I have heard enough stories to know I never want to. Like people, bears are fiercely protective of their cubs. They are attentive, caring, playful, and loving. They are advocates. I knew this is what I needed to be for my daughter. A fierce but respectful advocate. I would no longer walk away with my head down ashamed that I was too afraid to speak up in meetings. I know more about my daughter than any other human in this world and you know more about your child than any other human. One of the best pieces of advice my mother ever gave me was to follow my gut. I find more often than not, when I follow my gut, I make the best choices.

Nobody will truly understand your darkness unless they've walked in your shoes. As much as I try to explain and share my stories with loved ones, they really cannot understand the depth of my pain in dealing with my daughter's mental health conditions. It would be equivalent to me trying to understand the depth of a mother's sadness after losing a child. I might think I understand the pain, but I don't, as I have never lost a child.

It is important for you to let go of any anger or resentment you might have when loved ones make comments that make you feel alone and not understood. They are trying their hardest to understand and help. I find it most helpful to thank them for their support and silently tell myself they are sharing the best advice they know given they've never raised a child with a mood disorder. Later, I will give you tools and resources to use when you are feeling misunderstood and alone. I will also teach you the importance of building your tribe in Chapter 10. Your tribe will include other moms who are walking this same journey because these are the people who will understand your pain, fear, and feeling alone more than your friends or family.

The more open you are to sharing your story and struggles as a mom dealing with a child with a mood disorder, the more you will realize you are not alone and you are not failing. I fought to get a diagnosis for my child for years and I fought to get her help. I listened to one therapist after another tell me it was "typical" teenage behavior. Drinking, vaping, smoking marijuana and sneaking out of the house and walking across town from 1:00 to 5:00 a.m. were all considered typical teenage behavior. The problem was, my daughter was twelve at the time and in sixth grade. There was nothing typical about it.

I was terrified that my daughter would end up dead by high school from her high-risk behavior. My gut told me to keep on searching for the right therapist and doctors to work with us. My daughter's school staff also told me that she was doing "great," despite the fact that she was in a major depression, her grades were quickly falling, and she didn't have friends.

These are all examples of roadblocks. Get out your journal and keep a list of all the roadblocks you have overcome. That list right there is your proof that you are not failing as a mom! You can run into roadblocks at your child's school, therapist's office, doctor's office, and extracurricular activities. When the roadblock appears, you will release your inner mama bear. You know your child. You know what is typical and what is not typical. If it doesn't feel right, it isn't and you've hit a roadblock. Remember, that's OK. You know they will pop up periodically. Walk away and keep looking for the help your child needs and deserves. It's out there, I promise you, but it is not always easy to find.

Don't give up. The beauty about sharing your story with others is that they might have information that would be helpful in getting your child the help they need. I have already shared statistics with you. You know how prevalent mental illness is in our country. Every single person you will meet is either personally dealing with mental illness, has a family member with mental illness or has a friend with mental illness. You are never alone on this journey and most importantly, you are not failing. You are a warrior!

CHAPTER 6
STEP 3—LETTING IN LIGHT

· ·

"Hope is being able to see that there is light despite all of the darkness."

– Desmond Tutu

My Journal Entry August 8, 2004

She arrived! I can't believe I am a mom. I am still in a state of shock. I had this vision of what she would look like for nine months. A full head of black hair and olive skin. Imagine my surprise when she arrived with a full head of fire red hair! Two nurses cautioned me to "watch out" because of it. "She'll be feisty," warned a red-headed nurse with a laugh. I laughed along with her but ignored her advice. Looking down at my sweet baby girl, I knew there were no signs of feistiness. She was a tiny angel of pure perfection. As I looked into her eyes and held her close, I shared my hopes and dreams with her. I could not wait to see what life had in store for this little girl. I promised her I would be there for her, always and forever.

My Journal Entry June 14, 2019

I have been holding my breath. Olivia is in crisis. Her mental illnesses have paralyzed her. She keeps spiraling further down. Today, I was staring into her eyes as she lay next to me, and I imagined her as the baby I held on the day she was born. She was perfect. I remind myself that she still is "perfect" in an imperfect world. The hopes and dreams I had for her as a baby are no longer realistic. Honestly, I don't think they would be realistic for any child. I tell myself that I can let her have her own hopes and dreams, and I can support her by coaching her to discover healthy goals and dreams. She's lost right now. She can't think of goals. That's OK I tell myself. Someday she will.

We toured two therapeutic residential schools today. She needs round-the-clock support. Walking into the residential programs brought me relief, worry, sadness, and once again, a sense of failure as a mom.

At the same time, I know it's what my child needs to move forward. I have always imagined the day my daughters leave home for college and how sad I will be to say goodbye. I never imagined dropping my child off at a residential therapeutic school at age fourteen and saying goodbye, not knowing how long she would be gone for. I feel cheated out of these years. The kids here come from broken homes, abusive situations, trauma, heartache, and abandonment. How can my daughter be here? Mental illness is cruel. My heart aches.

It takes strength and courage as a mom to do what you know is right for your child. My daughter is angry. We walk out of the first residential program, and she starts screaming and swearing at me. She's pissed that her summer will be ruined. As much as I know it is not my fault, I listen to her. I validate. I take a deep breath. Deep down inside, I know the anger my child feels for me right this very minute will turn into love later tonight and then anger again. That's her mood disorder. Unpredictable, hurtful, confusing, sad, devastating, and cruel. But sometimes her mood disorder is loving, funny, sweet, and charming. I have learned to embrace those moments of tenderness. She holds me tight, tells me she loves me so much, and I feel and hold on to the love that she is offering. That's my girl.

Acceptance

When I was first introduced to the idea of acceptance, I was admittedly confused. Why would I accept my daughter's mood disorder? I won't accept her rude behavior toward me or her rages. I won't accept her irrational demands. In a way, I felt like accepting her illness would mean I would be giving up and giving in to her unacceptable behavior. I needed someone to help fix her and change her. I did not need to accept this.

As time went on, I realized this wasn't going to go away. Medication made her somewhat better after much trial and error, and therapy was helpful. But I came to realize that she would always be fighting these demons. There were no quick fixes. Her journey was one filled with baby steps. One step forward and one step back. When you accept something, it does not mean you like or agree with it, but you are allowing it to be, as you know you can't change it. You allow yourself to feel sad, fearful, worried, and disappointed. I realized when I accepted my daughter's diagnoses, my pain was far less than when I fought or rejected it. By rejecting her diagnoses, I was in fact, in a way, rejecting her, and it was causing her and me more suffering and pain.

Practicing acceptance is not easy. I had to practice acceptance of my daughter and her mental illnesses along with kindness toward myself. After all, I had been thinking about my daughter's hopes and dreams since the day she was born. It was not easy to put these aside and accept that she would never accomplish these things. I like to think of acceptance as a process. I came to understand that by accepting my daughter's mood disorder, it didn't mean I had to throw in the towel and give up. I still could be there for her and work with her treatment team to make progress toward her goals and her dreams. Once I let go of the "hopes and dreams" I had for her and realized I should help her discover her own hopes and dreams for herself, I felt a sense of relief.

When you think of acceptance, think about what other options you have if you don't accept your child's mood disorder. If you don't accept it, you reject it, and by rejecting something, you will cause pain and a decrease in happiness. When I fought to change my daughter and have her be like other girls her age, I was depressed and angry. When I accepted her and her illnesses, I felt at peace and happy.

True acceptance is understanding that something positive will come from every situation if you allow it to. If you try to find the goodness in the situation, you will be at peace and be able to move on. For years and years, I prayed that my daughter would get better, but much to my dismay she got worse. My heart physically ached. I just could not accept it. Until one day I realized I had no choice, but to accept it.

Mindfulness

Mindfulness helped me let go of judgment, focus on the now, and practice acceptance. As soon as I did that—and boy did it take practice—I saw my daughter and our situation in a different, more positive way. I started telling myself, "Something good will come out of this darkness," and day by day, darkness faded and light started shining through.

Just What Is Mindfulness and Why Is It Beneficial?

Mindfulness is the act of being fully present and aware of where we are and what we are doing. When we live mindfully we let go of judgment and free ourselves from distraction. We stop living in autopilot. We will still face challenges and uncomfortable situations when we practice mindfulness, but we might respond to these situations more calmly and empathetically. Living mindfully means living moment-by-moment fully aware of our thoughts, feelings, and surroundings.

"She is doing the best she can in this moment." These words are important to remember. Just when I think my daughter is failing or a disaster, I remind myself that she is doing the best she can, and if she could do better, she would. Those words bring me comfort, knowing this isn't my fault or her fault. We are both doing the best we can. Parents are not trained on how to handle a child with a mental illness. Children are not trained on how to live with one.

My daughter's doctor recently reminded me of the progress she has made. It is not groundbreaking progress, but baby steps leading into the right direction. I think back to where we started from, and I remember how horrific it was, how lost I was as a mom, and how lost she was as a child. It's not to say life is perfect now and she is healed. It is not. There are still dark days and moments, but within those dark days, I am able to see the light, even if it's just small glimmers.

We take baby steps. We focus on the now. We are mindful. We are patient. We love and cherish the one minute of the day where she might say, "I love you, Mommy" just like she did when she was two. I hold on to those tender moments because five minutes later, she could come back and say, "I hate you, Tanya, you are the worst mother ever." This is what a mood disorder does. It's ugly. But it is our reality. I have learned to accept it. I quietly celebrate the small steps, the progress, and the minor, little things that an outsider most likely would not notice.

How can we practice mindfulness as a parent and how can we introduce it to our child? Mindfulness is everywhere. Schools, homes, hospitals, offices, and extracurricular activities are practicing mindfulness. But why? What is this fascination with mindfulness? Research shows that mindfulness has positive effects on mental health and wellness. It has been shown to reduce stress and help people learn how to regulate emotions, become more compassionate and empathetic, and let go of judgment. Mindfulness has helped children and adults with anxiety, stress, ADHD, anger, and depression, just to name a few.

Mindfulness has helped me cope as a parent with a child with mental illness, and it has helped her cope with living with mental illness. When my daughter feels like she is losing control, or when I feel like I am losing control as her parent, we use the techniques we have learned in our mindfulness practice. We are able to reset and focus on the now while letting go of judgment.

Ways to Practice Mindfulness at Home

- **Five-minute brain break, breathing in the moment**: There are so many deep breathing exercises that can help you and your child self-regulate. There are apps that can guide you on breathing in the moment.

- **Smell in your favorite flower and breathe out a mountain or candle:** This is a favorite in my house. It helps us re-center and focus on the moment by using imagery and breath. Imagine one of your hands is the flower and the other hand is the mountain or candle. Take a deep breath in for three counts, smelling the flower in your left hand. What type of flower is it? What does it smell like? What color is it? Next, exhale for five counts, blowing out the candle or blowing out the "mountain." If your child is younger they may love using "candle breaths." What child doesn't love blowing out the candles on a birthday cake? When my daughter was younger, we liked to use my finger as a candle, and with exhale, the candle flame (my finger) would start to extinguish, which my child could visualize when my finger went from straight up to curled up.

- **The silence game**: The silence game can be done in any time increment you wish. One minute is a good starting point. Set a timer for one minute and sit as quietly as you can, focusing on what you see and hear in your surroundings. This activity will allow you to feel present and centered.

- **Drawing your emotions**: Many times, children are unable to name the emotions they are feeling. So, drawing their emotions is a great alternative

- **Taking five to ten deep, mindful breaths**: With a hand on your belly, take a deep breath in on the count of three. Watch your belly expand. Next, exhale deeply for a count of five and watch the air leave your belly. Mindful breathing is an easy way for you or your child to calm down and practice mindfulness wherever you are.

- **Noticing five things or hearing five things**: Look around and notice your surroundings. Name five things that you see or five things you hear. By noticing your surroundings, you will become focused on the present allowing yourself to let go of anxiety and reset.

- **Dropping anchor**: Stand with your feet firmly cemented on the floor, shoulder width apart. With your feet pushing into the floor, notice how your legs feel. How do your arms, toes, fingers, head, and muscles feel? Next, notice your surroundings.

Mindfulness includes awareness of the world that we live in. As you continue to stand with feet firmly planted on the ground, what do you hear? What do you see?

- **Nature walks:** Nature walks are my favorite! You will be amazed at how much you take in by being mindful on your walks. What do you see? What do you hear? What do you smell? You can also do "nature sitting" by sitting on a chair in your backyard and asking these same questions. You may be surprised by the overwhelming feeling of gratitude you will start to feel toward things we often take for granted. You may begin noticing things you haven't noticed on your walks in the past, as being mindful allows you to focus on your surroundings.

- **Talking about gratitude:** There have been many studies on the benefits of practicing gratitude. Decreased stress and anxiety, improved overall health and increased happiness are all benefits of practicing gratitude.

The Stages of Grief

The original five stages of grief have been updated and now include two additional stages, the shock and testing stages. People often think of grief as a process one goes through after the death of a loved one. I recognized that

I was going through stages of grief after my daughter was diagnosed with mental health illnesses and was in crisis.

The reality of our situation finally hit me after my daughter failed to make it at a program at one of the best mental health hospitals in the country. One of her doctors stated that she was "an extremely challenging kid." I finally realized that this wasn't just going to go away. That this really wasn't a parenting issue. That this really wasn't anyone's fault. I grieved. I sobbed. I realized the daughter I thought I gave birth to was not the daughter I had. My hopes and dreams for her were no longer realistic.

I sat and thought about these hopes and dreams I had for her. Were they really hopes and dreams for her, or were they hopes and dreams I had for myself, or my younger self? Shouldn't my hopes and dreams for my daughter be good health, happiness, love, and finding a job that she is passionate about? I started realizing that I had to let go of the hopes and dreams I had when she was born. I had to grieve those dreams. I had to grieve that little infant that I held on August 8, 2004.

The process of grieving allows you to enter into a new stage of your life without holding back. It may seem very scary at first. It was for me. You may be stalling your grieving if you are hanging on to the hopes and dreams you had for your child when they were born. Let go of those hopes and dreams. Can you think of more realistic hopes and dreams for your child? Or, perhaps you can allow your child to make their own realistic hopes and dreams. Take the first step toward grieving and feel the sense of relief flood over your body. You will feel a sense of calmness and relief as you begin the process of grieving. Remember, you are not alone on this journey. You will learn in a later chapter how you will build your tribe, and your tribe will help you through the stages of grief.

The Seven Stages of Grief:

1. *Shock.* The realization that my daughter's anger, rage, tantrums, and inability to go to school were part of a mental illness. Bad news. I was paralyzed. I couldn't express emotions.

2. *Denial.* I tried to tell myself that maybe this would get better. Maybe she would outgrow it. Maybe the doctor was wrong.

3. *Anger.* This is my husband's fault. This is my fault. I never should have had a baby. How could this be?

4. *Bargaining.* Lots of bargaining went on, but that never helped. Things didn't get better.

5. *Depression.* I was in a definite funk for a period of time, especially when I saw girls my daughter used to be friends with. They were accomplished and seemed like perfect girls.

6. *Testing.* I have been in this stage many, many times. Hunting for solutions. Trying to fix her. Trying to find ways to help her.

7. *Acceptance.* Finding a way to move forward, not backward. When you get to this stage, you know you will be OK. Even if every day you feel like you might not be OK, trust me, you will be.

These are the stages that you will go through. As you go through them, you will begin to accept, heal, surrender, rediscover love, and find happiness within yourself and your child. There is no order to the stages. You might jump from one to another, which is perfectly acceptable. That is how grief works. Be open to the process and trust it.

You now know the steps you will need to take to allow the light to start shining through on this difficult journey of raising a child with a mood disorder. Acceptance is not easy, but you will be amazed at the shift you will feel from sadness, fear, and disappointment to happiness, peace, and pride just by accepting your child for the person he or she was born to be. To allow for the change you will feel after you accept your child and their diagnosis, practicing mindfulness is critical to help you continue on this journey in a positive and healthy way. Start slowly. You can build on your mindfulness practice each week. Be gentle and kind to yourself. These are big changes and may seem foreign to you as you get started. That is to be expected. Getting into the habit of any new practice takes time, patience, and commitment.

Lastly, as you go through the stages of grief, you will be practicing mindfulness and acceptance. Again, be kind to yourself. Allow yourself to feel the emotions. With time, you will begin to feel the happiness that is tucked deep in your soul and that is when you will know the light is beginning to shine through the darkness.

CHAPTER 7
STEP 4—LET'S BUILD A TOOLBOX

· ·

"When you can't control what's happening, challenge yourself to control the way you respond to what's happening. That's where the power is!"

— Unknown

Journal Entry—April 28, 2019

A fire is burning deep in my belly. I try to breathe through the excruciating feeling of losing hope that my daughter will get what she needs at school. I sit at the table at Olivia's Individualized Education Program meeting, looking at faces of grown adults who know so little about my daughter yet have the power to make decisions that will affect her for life. I am shaking uncontrollably. I can't stop.

For years, I have fought for my daughter's rights at school. There were times in the earlier days when I sat silently listening to them speak inaccurately about my daughter, just to avoid confrontation. After those meetings, I would walk out of the school and beat myself up for not speaking up. I hated confrontation. I accepted the mistruths that the school personnel would speak. "Your daughter is doing great," they'd say. She was not great nor was she fine. She was quietly suffering and spiraling down, calling out for help. If we didn't catch her now, she'd be addicted to drugs and involved in even more high-risk activities by ninth grade and on the path to dropping out of high school.

I feel like I have been punched in the stomach again. My daughter's needs are so great. Deep down, the school knows this, but it has a budget and my daughter's needs far outweigh it. But by law they are required to accommodate her at school. I no longer care about offending school personnel by defending my daughter's rights. I am a mama bear and will do anything and everything to provide for my daughter. As I walk out of the meeting, I continue to shake. I cannot stop. The stress, anxiety, and fear take over my body. I have no control. I reach my car, open the door, slide

into my seat, and allow the tears to come. Still shaking,
I reach into my back seat and grab my "calming box."

Overview

This chapter will be filled with tools and activities
that you can use in times of emotional distress to provide
comfort and offer a way to distract you, as well as resources
to offer you knowledge and support. These tools are both
tangible objects that you can use in a hands-on kit that you
make at home, often called a toolbox or a calming box, and
also activities and online resources to help arm you with
information and support on your journey. My hope is that
you will find these tools make your life less stressful and you
feel more supported.

What is a Toolbox or Calming Box?

Toolboxes or calming boxes are kits that you can make at
home that are filled with hands-on tools to help self-soothe
in times of emotional distress or anger. The items that you
put in the kit are customized to what you find helpful in
distracting or soothing yourself when you need help getting
grounded. Calming boxes are wonderful for both children
and adults in times of distress. Tangible objects help distract
and soothe. Using calming boxes can help children or adults
cope more effectively rather than give in to the urge to use
self-harm, self-medication, or angry outbursts to cope. I have
created three types of toolboxes for my family. I have my own

personal "mama bear" toolbox, each of my three daughters have their own toolbox, and we have a family toolbox.

Building a Personal Toolbox

One size does not fit all when it comes to creating a toolbox! You will have to experiment to find what tools work best for you or your child. Calming Boxes have always been a favorite way for my daughters to use hands-on strategies for self-soothing in times of emotional distress. The objects you add to your box should be items that you will find soothing and distracting in times of distress. Limit use of these items so you are only using them when you need to help regulate your emotions. The items in your calming box should not be items that you use in your everyday life.

Have fun building your calming box! This is a great activity to do with your child or as a family. Boxes can be made from shoe boxes and decorated with your favorite wrapping paper or pictures. Alternatively, you can pick up boxes at home stores or office supply stores that are already decorated. When building your box, think of all five senses and try to have at least one item for each sense. Many of the items you may already have at home, or you can find them at a local store. Some examples of items that you might add to your box include the following:

- Slime, stress balls, play dough, or molding sand
- Bubbles to blow out angry emotions

- Essential oils to help calm your mind and body
- Journal or coloring book and pencils
- Stuffed animal or small blanket
- A favorite candy or treat that you'll have only in the box (pick a favorite flavor like cherry and then choose cherry lollipops, gum, or hard candy)
- Book of meditations or affirmations
- Legos or small toy
- A photo of your favorite person or animal
- Healing stones and crystals
- Music

After you make your calming box, share what you put in your box with others and tell them how you will use it when you are feeling angry, sad, overwhelmed, stressed, or anxious. The items you add to your box should be tangible to allow for grounding yourself in times of distress. These items will provide you with comfort and also distract you.

Keep your journal handy and record your observations about your calming box after you use it. Was it helpful? Did you calm down more quickly? Did you scream less? Were your emotions more in check? Do you need to change any of the items in the box to make your box more effective? Remember, the purpose of the calming box is to help ground yourself in times of emotional distress. Your calming box can always be changed to suit your needs.

"Calming boxes help me manage my anger and anxiety. I keep one in my room and one at school. I like to switch up the tools when I need a change. I always keep at least one essential oil roller ball in my calming box. Scents calm me."

– **Alex**, age thirteen

Relaxation Techniques for Stress

Let's face it, raising children with mood disorders is unbelievably stressful. The more tools we have, the better we will be able to cope. The techniques below are tools you can use anytime and anywhere, so if you are out and don't have your calming box with you, use one of these techniques or download one of the recommended apps.

Body Scan

For this technique you will focus on your breath and muscle relaxation.

You will start by focusing on your breathing. As your body begins to sink down and relax, you are focusing on your breath. Focus on one part of the body at a time. I like to start with my head (eyes, mouth, jaw, tongue) and release any tension I may have in each of these areas. Body scans help you become more aware of the mind-body connection.

Mindful Meditation

Mindfulness meditation is helpful for people with depression, anxiety, and mood disorders. Find a comfortable spot and focus on your breathing. Focus on the present moment without thinking about the future or the past. Let go of all judgment and just stay in the moment. You may wish to play your own calming music or download a free mediation app or online meditation to help guide you. Start with five minutes of meditation and slowly increase the time each week. Remember, let go of judgments. If your mind wanders, be kind to yourself and refocus.

Guided Imagery

There are many free apps or resources online of recordings of calming scenes.

Think of scenes or places that will help you let go of stress and relax. The goal is to create a sense of calm in your mind. With a consistent meditation practice, you can improve your mood, sleep, focus, and happiness. You can also decrease blood pressure, anxiety, and irritability.

Some of my favorite apps to help reduce stress include:

- Unplug: Guided Meditation
- Breathe: Sleep & Meditation
- Relax Meditation
- Meditation and Relaxation

These are great at the end of the day, especially if stress is keeping you up at night!

More Recommended Tools

Here are more of my favorite tools for reducing stress and getting grounded. Essential oils can be used to aide in relaxation or to reduce stress. I have also used them to improve mental clarity when I am overtired. These essential oil rollers are so easy and fun to make and work wonderfully! If making them sounds like too much work, they can be purchased online or in stores. Essential oils are known to be highly therapeutic and have been used for centuries. They can create harmony in the body as well as peace in the mind. I have included some of my favorite recipes for calming your mind and body, reducing anxiety, and boosting your energy! I love to make these in roller bottles and roll on hands, feet, temples or wrists. One or two rolls on one area of your body is really all you need to melt the anxiety away, lower your stress, or give yourself an energy boost! Keep these handy in your purse, in the car, by your bed, or in your calming box.

Recipes for Essential Oils Roller Bottle

You'll need:

- 10 mL glass roller bottles (I like the metal roller balls)
- Carrier oils (my favorite is fractionated coconut oil, but I also use almond oil or avocado oil)

- Essential oils
- Plastic droppers to add the oils

These items can be purchased on Amazon.

Ground Yourself Formula
- Eight drops frankincense essential oil (for calming/grounding)
- Eight drops wild orange oil (uplifting and cleansing)
- Four drops Roman chamomile essential oil (soothing/calming)
- Fractionated coconut oil
- Roll on hands, wrists, temples, feet. Great for calming adults and kids!

Anti-Anxiety Formula
- Four drops frankincense essential oil
- Four drops marjoram essential oil
- Six drops geranium essential oil
- Six drops clary sage essential oil
- Four drops wild orange essential oil

Energize Formula
- Fourteen drops eucalyptus essential oil
- Ten drops rosemary essential oil
- Six drops grapefruit essential oil
- Great for a boost of energy in adults and kids!

Tools and Activities

Here are more of my favorite tools and activities for managing stress and handling big emotions. These all work equally well for adults and kids. Some of these will fit in your calming box, but others will be too big.

- **Weighted Blankets**: Blankets with weight evenly distributed can help calm and ground in times of distress. They can also be used at night to help provide a deep sleep
- **Weighted Vest**: Vests also help reduce anxiety and stress
- **Fidgets**: Purchase online or at local toy stores. Keep them in your purse, car, bedrooms
- **Yoga Balls:** Light bouncing will provide a calming effect

Calming Down Bottle

My children love to make these with me. We use clear plastic water bottles with the wide mouth (easier to fill). Peel off the label and use an empty water bottle. Purchase soft water beads from a craft store or online at Amazon. They are very small but when you add them to water (about one cup) and soak them for eight hours they will expand. Add your favorite colors to the bottle and add some water. These bottles have an immediate calming effect.

A-to-Z Activity

This activity can be done anywhere and anytime, such as in the car or waiting in a doctor's office, at school, at the office, or at home. It will help calm you and refocus your energy by focusing on the present. Look around your surroundings. Starting with the letter A, name one thing you see that begins with that letter. Move on to letter B and continue on until you reach letter Z.

Ten Details

This can also be done anyplace. Pause and take time to observe and describe ten details you would not otherwise have noticed.

Untie Knots

Shoelaces work great for this activity, or alternatively you can use a long piece of string. Take a shoelace or string that has knots or tangles in it. Staying in the present moment, untie the knots. If feelings come up, acknowledge them, breathe, and stay in the present as you complete this task.

Window Watching

Choose a window you rarely look out. Sit down and look out the window for five minutes. Notice what is outside the window. What is the scenery? Is there any activity going on? Describe in detail what you notice. Stay in the present moment. Release judgment about what you see. Stay mindful.

Favorite Apps
- Headspace: Meditation & Sleep
- Louise Hay Affirmations
- Calm: Meditation and Sleep Stories
- Insight Timer
- Stop, Breathe & Think
- 10% Happier
- Meditation Studio

Online Resources

There are an abundance of online resources that you can use to help manage the stress and anxiety mental illness can cause. These resources will also help you as you navigate your journey raising a child with a mood disorder. You will find support, additional tools, and a wealth of information on these online sites.

- NAMI—www.nami.org. The National Alliance on Mental Illness has more than five hundred local affiliates that work to raise awareness and provide resources and support to the millions of people affected by mental illness
- NFFCMH—www.ffcmh.org. National Federation of Families for Children's Mental Health is a national

family-run organization focused on the issues of children with emotional, behavioral, or mental health issues with over 120 chapters.

- NIMH—www.nimh.nih.gov. The National Institute of Mental Health is one of the institutes that make up the National Institutes of Health, the largest biomedical research agency in the world.

- MHA—www.mentalhealthamerica.net. Mental Health America was founded in 1909 and is the nation's leading community-based nonprofit dedicated to promoting mental health as a critical component of overall wellness. MHA is committed to providing support, services, and early identification for those at risk.

- MHF—www.mentalhealthfoundation.net. The Mental Health Foundation encourages early diagnosis and reducing stigma of mental illness. It also strives to improve understanding of mental illness and ensure access to quality care

Support Groups

Parenting or caring for a child with a mood disorder can be overwhelming and isolating. Joining a support group is a way for you to connect with other people who are going through similar situations. By sharing your experience, you'll be helping others and in turn, you will feel understood and less alone. Support groups will help you learn how to manage a crisis, take care of yourself, learn how to support your child, and advocate for your child at school and medical appointments. Check with your local mental health organizations to find support groups near you.

Support groups are also important for siblings of children with mental illness. Oftentimes, siblings are forgotten and left unsupported. As mothers, we are so busy caring for the child with the illness that the siblings are receiving less of our time, and they are often confused and scared about what is happening to their sibling. Mood disorders are so unpredictable and frequently, siblings are victims of attacks. It is critical to get siblings the support they need.

NAMI (www.nami.org) offers support groups. Find your local chapter online. NAMI Basics is a six-week class for parents or caregivers of children with behavioral or emotional issues. You are not alone on this journey and surrounding yourself with other parents who are on the same journey will help you feel validated and supported.

You can also search Facebook groups to find private support groups online. These groups are helpful if you have little time to travel outside of your home for weekly appointments. You'll find many online support groups for parenting children with mood disorders or mental illnesses.

School Support

This could be an entire book, but I will just touch on it for now. It is imperative that you advocate for your child at school and that they learn how to advocate for themselves. Children with mood disorders are at a high risk for school dropout in the high school years. They are also at a much higher risk for substance abuse. Children who have the appropriate support can thrive in school and learn how to develop meaningful relationships with peers and teachers. It takes a village to help children with mental health conditions be successful in school. The special education process is extremely complex, especially if the school is not working cooperatively with you, the parents.

If you feel your child is not getting the appropriate support at school and that they are falling behind, search for a special education advocate in your area to help you. It is well worth the time and money. Check with your child's psychologist, as many are well versed in special education law and are willing to serve as advocates. If not, search online for special education advocates. Schools are required by law to offer accommodations to students with mental health conditions. The following websites are good places to visit for guidance with support related to school issues.

- NAMI.org has information for parents on how to navigate the special education process in schools.
- wrightslaw.com is a website you should bookmark. Lawyers, parents, advocates, and school personnel use this site for reliable information on special

education laws. You will find thousands of articles and resources in the online library at Wrightslaw.

- specialeducationguide.com is a great resource for parents that outlines your child's legal rights. Special education laws are described in layman's terms. The steps you need to take as a parent to get the services your child with a mental illness, by law, is entitled to, are clearly laid out with a timeline in this guide.

We have covered a lot of information in this chapter! Don't let it overwhelm you! I recommend starting by building a calming box with your child. Each week, you can try new activities or tools. Take note of what works well for you and have a conversation with your child about what they find helpful. You are both building new skills that will help you manage emotions. Keep your journals handy so you remember your favorites and watch your progress.

CHAPTER 8

STEP 5—NEGATIVE SELF-TALK NOT ALLOWED

. . . .

"Train your mind to see the good in everything. Positivity is a choice. The happiness of your life depends on the quality of your thoughts."

– marcandangel

My Journal Entry—August 26, 2016

The phone call I have been waiting for arrived today. When I heard my doctor's voice on the other end, I knew the news wasn't good. "Hi, Tanya, I am calling to confirm that you have breast cancer." She continued to talk, but her words started slurring together. I eventually stopped listening to her and started listening to the voice in my head. "Oh, crap, I have cancer! I am going to die! I'll never see my daughters graduate, get married, or have babies." Losing my mother to cancer just years before, I knew all too well the pain and suffering that cancer can cause. I hung up the phone and broke down and cried.

Survivor

I am happy to report that I am a breast cancer survivor and to help me through my journey, I used positive affirmations every single day. I allowed myself to cry and have my "poor me" moments that very first day and then I told myself that I would have to change my thoughts and become positive. In order for me to make this journey as seamless as possible, I would have to train my brain to have my thoughts and words be positive. Once I was able to let go of my fear and embrace positive affirmations, I was able to train my mind for a positive breast cancer journey. Now, that's not to say that there were not parts of the journey that weren't hard or miserable. There were, but when those moments came, I was better equipped to handle them. What I learned and implemented on my breast cancer journey, I was able to transfer to my journey of parenting my child with a mood disorder.

Positive Affirmations

We all know the power of positive thinking, so why is it so hard to think positively when we are living in the midst of a crisis? What can we do to change our thinking? What is the first step we can take? My mother used to say to me, "When one door closes, another will always open." That little change in my thinking got me through high school breakups and many other disappointments. In essence, she was helping me train my brain, by shifting my thinking and creating positive thoughts. If you are at work, listen in to the conversations at lunch. I bet, more often than not, you will hear negative statements more often than positive. In order to make changes in our lives, we need to train our brain to think and speak using positive statements.

The journey with a child who has a mood disorder or other mental illness is challenging and one would certainly expect it to be more negative than positive, but ultimately, the choice is yours, as this is your journey. Ask yourself these questions. Can you dig deep down and find the positives in your child and focus on these positives? Or will you dwell on the negatives and let the mood disorder overcome your life? I have done both and I will tell you, when I started to focus on the positives, my life started to turn around. I rediscovered who I was as a mother and woman. When you begin to think positively about your child's mood disorder, you'll be on the path of acceptance. Days with my daughter are still incredibly challenging. Her mood disorder has not gone away. She is still the same child who is frequently demanding, angry, aggressive, and mean. But the way my mind views her mood disorder has changed.

A Text from My Daughter

>   Her: Mom, I need you to take me to the ER I really hurt
>   my ankle
>
>   Me: OK, I will come get you, how did it happen?
>
>   Her: Where are you taking me?
>
>   Me: Urgent care
>
>   Her: I'm so pissed off at this family. No, just leave me
>   alone
>
>   Me: What?
>
>   Her: I'm so annoyed leave me alone
>
>   Me: So you don't want to get your ankle checked?
>
>   Her: I'm so upset you don't even understand

A few minutes pass…

>   Her: Pick me up, I need to go to urgent care

Ten minutes later, I pick her up and she gives me a huge hug and tells me she loves me.

Twenty minutes later, she is swearing at me in the exam room as we wait for the doctor. She is irritated because I asked her to remover her sock so the doctor could check her ankle. This is a mood disorder.

You may be at the beginning of your journey with a child with a mood disorder or you may be years into it. A mood disorder can be so confusing and unpredictable. One minute, your child may be on a rage and the next minute, they're telling you they love you. When my daughter yells and swears at me, I don't react. I remind myself that she lacks skills and has a mood disorder. I remind myself that she is getting help and we have the best team in place for her to work on skill building and managing her emotions. When things get very disruptive and she is hurtful, I remember to breathe and take steps to take care of myself. So, what are these steps?

Mindfulness

In Chapter 6, I introduced mindfulness to you. We talked about the benefit of a mindfulness practice in regulating emotions and how to build a practice at home! I discovered mindfulness years ago as a way to manage my emotions and tolerate distress. I was pleasantly surprised to discover that mindfulness also improved my quality of life. Building my mindfulness practice allowed me to find respite from the darkness of my daughter's mood disorder. It can help build strength and offer hope to an otherwise hopeless situation.

We all feel stress, but how we deal with stress differs from person to person. Stress in itself is not bad, as it can help you take action and stay focused. But, stress can also cause immense suffering if it depletes ones mental, emotional, and physical reserves. I have seen this in my own health, dealing with several autoimmune conditions and cancer. Shortly after my cancer diagnosis, I cultivated a mindfulness approach and became more proactive, which helped me manage stress before it manifested in my body.

The first step in cultivating a mindfulness practice is carving out the time just for you each day. This was hard for me, as I am a mother to three busy girls, who all have significant health needs. As mothers, we are programed to think we don't deserve free time. By nature, we are nurturers. We give to others and neglect our own needs. We must recognize that we can be caregivers without neglecting our needs. Once I realized that my health would benefit if I took care of myself first, I was able to become an even better mother. My stress was lower, I was able to tolerate unexpected events better, my emotions were more in check, and I had more energy.

My mindfulness practice began by committing to five minutes a day. I called these my "Mini Mindfulness Mediations for Mom." Many of my earlier mindfulness sessions were in my car during school pickup. I would arrive at the school at least fifteen minutes early to give myself that time to get centered before the girls got in my car. It was one of the few quiet places I found that would give me uninterrupted time to be mindful. There are thousands of mindful activities and meditations online for free. Some are brief and some are longer, so you can start with the shorter activities and build up as your practice grows stronger.

Five-Minute Mindfulness Activities

Mindful Breathing

I will address breathing in more depth in the next chapter, but for now, start to work on your breath. Focusing on your breath will help calm your mind and body. In a quiet space, close your eyes and begin to focus on your breath. Let your body relax and just breathe. Let go of any thoughts. Release any judgments. Notice any tension in your body and let it go. Continue to focus on your breath. In this activity, you will focus on the natural rhythm of your breath. As you breathe in and out, feel the warmth of your breath when you breathe through your nostrils and through your mouth. Notice where you feel your breath (nostrils, chest, or abdomen.) As you are focusing on your breath, you may begin to feel your mind wander. This is normal and will inevitably happen. Be kind to yourself and acknowledge that your mind has wandered. Then, refocus your attention back to your breath. Before ending this mindfulness activity, check in with yourself. Is your body more relaxed? Is your mind calm? Show yourself some appreciation for spending five minutes taking care of yourself.

The Five Senses

You can do this activity anytime and anywhere. Its purpose is to bring attention to each of your five senses, which will allow you to focus on the present moment. This mindfulness exercise will help ground you in times of stress. Prior to starting, notice your breathing, heart rate, and body. How do you feel? Do you feel out of control? Lost? Overwhelmed? Find a quiet space and take five minutes to do the following exercise.

Sit in a relaxed position with your feet on the ground. Close your eyes and begin to focus on your breath. Inhale and exhale fully. One at a time, for approximately one minute each, you will focus on each of the five senses. This is not a time of judgment. You will be observing using your five senses in the moment, but you will not be judging.

To start, open your eyes and look around. Find five things that you can see. Notice the color and texture of the objects you see.

Next, listen for four things that you can hear. Continue to inhale and exhale as you focus on your hearing. What are four sounds that you can hear? Did you notice these sounds before you started this exercise?

After that, feel three things that can be touched. What do the objects feel like? Remember, you are not judging. If your mind wanders, you can bring it back to the exercise. Do not judge yourself or get frustrated.

Next, find two things that you can smell. Notice the smells around you. Maybe you are outside and can smell fresh grass cut or flowers.

Lastly, find one thing that you can taste. If you have food near you take a bite and notice what you taste. If you don't have food, think about what your mouth tastes like.

At the end of the activity, notice how you feel. Are you grounded? Has your breathing slowed down? Did your heart-rate slow down? Do you feel better equipped to deal with problems that you might be having?

Mindful Awareness

Think of something you do several times a day. It might be something that you take for granted. For example, I go on walks with my dogs more than once a day. Many times, I am rushing to get the dogs out so I can get to the next item on my list. On my walk, when I am mindful, I stay in the moment and notice my environment. I notice the temperature outside, birds chirping, other people or dogs walking, flowers and green grass. Staying mindful on my walks helps to calm me down. My focus shifts from what is coming up next to the present. I am able to appreciate the now and enjoy the time with my dogs. My heart rate slows down, my anxiety goes away and I am calm. I am ready to tackle the next item on my list. You can do this same exercise at work, at home, in your car, or outside. The possibilities are endless.

When we intentionally devote at least five minutes of time to a daily mindfulness practice, we create awareness and foster inner peace. Once you begin to appreciate the little things in life, you will find more joy throughout your day. Your focus will shift from the negative and you will begin to embrace the positive. Our lives are often hectic and filled with stress. Many of us go nonstop all day on autopilot. Taking time each day to be mindful will remind you of what is important and how to manage the stress of your day-to-day life.

Therapy

Many people I talk to about therapy have a love-hate relationship with it. I have always been a firm believer in therapy. I started going twenty years ago. I take breaks when needed and change therapists when I feel I need a change. The key is finding what works for you. If you meet a therapist and don't feel comfortable, try a few more times before determining if it is a good fit. If it is not, they won't have hard feelings when you decide to try someone new. A skilled therapist, especially one who is very familiar with mood disorders, can help you learn how to cope with your emotions and effectively parent your child. The right therapist will validate your feelings. Validation is a beautiful feeling. My therapist is a pro at it and I always leave her office feeling supported and understood.

Therapists can also teach you how to use self-validation effectively. It takes practice! Recognizing and accepting your own feelings and thoughts as understandable is an important step on your journey of parenting a child with a mood disorder. When you are on this journey day in and out, it becomes critical to self-validate yourself as a mother. The negative talk must go. It is time to embrace the positive and learn how to love yourself unconditionally. Release judgment of yourself. Release judgment that others may have said about you. I like to say the following affirmations when I am feeling like I am failing as a mother:

- I am enough
- I am OK
- When I start hearing myself say, "I can't do it," I quickly say, "I can do it, I am doing it!"
- I am in charge of how I feel, and today I am choosing happiness
- I can. I will.
- I will not compare myself to other mothers who are not on this journey
- I am whole
- I have the power to create change
- I am calm, happy, and content
- I am more at ease every day
- I deserve to have joy in my life

Journaling

I have already mentioned journaling many times because it offers many benefits. There are so many fun, colorful, and inspirational journals available, or if you prefer, you can always type on your computer! There are times when I am driving that I "journal" by talking into my phone to create a note. Journaling is therapeutic and helps to reduce stress and promote emotional healing. It is also a great tool for self-reflection. I have learned more about myself as a mother through journaling than anything else. I tend to write mostly when I am undergoing a stressful time with my daughter. I grab my pen when I feel like I can't make it through the day. I find writing about my emotions and processing the problem allows me to cope with the stress and explore other options for dealing with the crisis. In my earlier days of journaling, I noticed my writing was filled with more negatives than positives. Through mindfulness practice, I learned to focus on the positives and stop judging. I noticed my writing changed and I was more open to self-validation and acceptance. If you can do this, your relationship with yourself and your child will change.

Schedule Time for Self-Care

Scheduling time for yourself is a must. At a minimum, take five minutes a day to practice mindfulness. Put these five minutes into your calendar. It has to be scheduled, just like you would schedule any other appointment. Each week, I schedule my workouts and put them in my calendar. I also schedule time for therapy, acupuncture, meditation, and Reiki. I make sure to fit in a manicure/pedicure and a hair appointment each month. What are things you can do to take care of your mental and physical health each week?

The most important thing you can do, for yourself or your child, is to be kind to yourself. Find time to take care of yourself each day, and acknowledge and allow yourself to feel your emotions. Once I accepted and learned that self-care was critical for me as a mom, I noticed my patience with my daughter increased, my energy increased, and my moods improved. I began to believe that her mood disorder was not my fault and I was doing the best I knew how to be a good mother to her. This made all the difference in the world in how I viewed myself and her. My thoughts and comments shifted from negative to positive and I became happier.

As I learned how to love myself and her in a whole new way, I was able to let go of the disappointment, shame, embarrassment, and anger I felt as a mother to a daughter with severe mental health issues. I opened my heart to allow healing, love, acceptance, understanding, and pride. I began seeing my daughter's illnesses in a new light. Stress melted away as acceptance took over. I began to see the blessing she has always been.

CHAPTER 9

STEP 6—EVERY LITTLE THING WILL BE OK, BREATHE!

. . . .

"The quality of our breath expresses our inner feelings"
– TKV Desikachar

My Journal Entry—December 23, 2018

Three, two, one ... I can breathe. One thousand pounds of bricks lifted off me seconds after hearing four words: "You daughter has DMDD [disruptive mood dysregulation disorder]." Relief. What would be devastating news for most moms is not to me because for years, I have been searching for the answer for her intense mood swings and raging tantrums. We have been in and out of specialists, therapists, behavior specialists, psychologists, and psychiatrists, day after day, year after year, fighting to find the answer. Holding on to hope that I could help my little red-haired, blue eyed girl. This became my life mission, my full-time job. I knew there was hope and I promised myself I would not give up until I found her help and an answer. For the first time in twelve years, I feel like I can let some of the stress and anxiety go. I can stop focusing on every little thing and breathe again. I can accept that I am a good mom. I am not a failure. I don't have to compare my daughter to other girls her age. She is different. My daughter has a mental illness that makes her atypical but not in a bad way. She is smart, beautiful, funny, talented, and sweet. Sometimes she hides these traits, but I know they are there. I have seen them. They come and go but they are deep inside her. Throughout our journey together, as mother and daughter, searching for answers, we have learned that we have to slow down, accept the reality, embrace the moment, and just breathe.

Learning How to Breathe

For years, I have been holding my breath without even knowing. Through my mindfulness practice, I began noticing that I was not breathing properly. I never understood the importance of proper breathing until my trainer explained it to me. Diaphragmatic breathing (belly breathing) has many health benefits, reducing stress being one of the biggest ones. Other benefits include lowering blood pressure, decreasing heart rate, helping you relax, and lowering the harmful effects of cortisol, a stress hormone, on your body.

When a person is under stress, the immune system is not working fully, which can make you more susceptible to health problems. Diaphragmatic breathing is used in almost all meditation techniques. Learning to control your breath will bring you many health benefits, and will be well worth your time. I find it to be a tool I use over and over when I need to self-regulate. Your breath is always with you, and it's a tool that will come in handy. Learning this technique is not difficult. It just takes time and practice!

Diaphragmatic Breathing Instructions

1. Sit or lie flat in a comfortable position.
2. Relax your body, letting go of any stress in your shoulders.
3. Place a hand on your stomach and a hand on your chest.
4. Breathe in through your nostrils for two counts. The air flowing through your nostrils will make your abdomen expand. Your chest should remain still as your abdomen expands.

5. With your lips pursed as though you are drinking through a straw, exhale slowly for two counts while gently pressing on your abdomen.
6. Repeat for ten to twenty minutes.
7. Try to do this exercise one or two times each day.

I'm OK!

My closest friends know that one of my favorite personal mantras is "I'm OK." When I feel like I am at my lowest point as a mother, I repeat the words to myself over and over, "I'm OK." I also used this repeatedly during my breast cancer journey, and it worked for both emotional and physical pain.

During my darkest and most painful days as a mother to a child with a mood disorder, I often felt like I could not take another step forward. I wanted to give up and throw in the towel, over and over, because I felt like a failure and thought my daughter deserved better. Many times, I would drop to my knees and repeat, "I'm OK." My mind calmed and I became "OK" or "fine." This also worked for the physical pain of breast cancer. During excruciating pain, I would tell myself "I'm OK," and my mind calmed, my body relaxed, and I tolerated the pain.

Find your own personal mantra to help motivate you to be your best self. Maybe you already have a favorite mantra or maybe you've heard other people use mantras that resonate with you, but you haven't tried using them for yourself. See what feels right, make a list, and start trying a few out. If you are having trouble finding one that resonates with you, head to your local library or bookstore and pick up a book on mantras. This is something that you can do quickly and easily to shift your thinking.

Some of my favorite mantras are
- Breathe.
- Forward progress, just keep moving.
- I am enough.
- I am strong. I am brave.
- I am doing my best. That is all I can expect of myself.
- This too shall pass.
- My child is doing the best he or she can right now.

Other Recommendations to Help Calm Your Body and Improve Your Breath

Reiki

Reiki is a form of hands-on energy healing originating in Japan. It is used to help reduce stress and promote relaxation, as well as physical and emotional healing. I discovered Reiki after my mastectomy while I was in the hospital. I received a treatment from a Reiki volunteer, and it allowed me to go into a full relaxation. Many hospitals now offer Reiki post-surgery or during cancer treatments. It has helped me become more centered, less reactive, and less stressed. It has also brought much balance to my life and fills me with contentment. I was so impressed with my individual results, I decided to become a Reiki practitioner shortly after my mastectomy. During my Reiki sessions, I focus on my breath and repeat a mantra that speaks to me during the session.

Creating a Wellness Room

One day, I was sitting in my office, and after looking around, decided I needed to spruce it up a bit. I needed a safe, calm space where my children and I could go to practice mindfulness, pause, rest, breathe, and just be. I chose calming colors and outfitted my office with a massage table for Reiki or relaxation, cozy chairs, candles, and essential oils. Books of affirmations and mindfulness can be found throughout. A wellness room could not be complete without fidgets (my daughters' favorite calming tool), my own calming box, and mantras. It is a safe space where we can come to be present in the moment.

When I am feeling overwhelmed and need space, I go into my wellness room and ask myself, "What do I need?" I listen to my body, tune in, and discover what I need for self-care right now. I honor my body and allow myself the time to get centered. This is also the space I "run" to when I am feeling overwhelmed as a mom in times of chaos. The trick to surviving the chaos is to choose how to respond to it rather than reacting. Take time to just be. Sit alone. Be mindful. Be kind. Be still. Breathe. Repeat your favorite mantra.

Moms in Their Own Words

"When I learned to stop worrying about things in the future, my mind calmed down and I was able to start focusing on the now. Mindfulness helped me be present for my child."

"Practicing mindfulness allowed me to focus on my breath and create a calm space. Things I found overwhelming became manageable."

"I allow myself to feel the emotions I feel when I feel them. I acknowledge them, accept them, and then move on."

"I learned that taking care of myself was a necessity, not a luxury. My child was much happier when I became more grounded."

Take this time to pause and take out your journal. Make notes of any mantras that may have resonated with you and make a goal of how many times a week you will commit to practicing your breathing. Do you have a space in your home where you can create a wellness room or nook? Think about things that would bring you comfort and offer you hope that you truly are "OK!"

CHAPTER 10

STEP 7—SUPPORT LOOKS LIKE THIS: BUILDING A SISTERHOOD OR TRIBE

. . . .

"The realization that we are all basically the same human beings who seek happiness and try to avoid suffering is very helpful in developing a sense of brotherhood and sisterhood; a warm feeling of love and compassion for others."

– Dalai Lama

My Journal Entry—February 5, 2019

For years, I have been talking to myself, writing in journals, and sharing my thoughts and fears about my daughter's mental illnesses with friends and loved ones. It's comforting to know that I have a tribe who will always be there for me to listen and offer support. I've always been grateful for their unconditional love. However, it wasn't until today that I realized what I really needed was to talk to someone who is experiencing exactly what I am experiencing, another mom who also has a daughter with a mood disorder, anxiety, and other comorbid illnesses. Today, by the grace of God, I talked to "Linda" (named changed to protect her identity.)

Linda was another mom in our family dialectical behavior therapy group at one of the leading psychiatric hospitals. Linda and I never sat near each other and opportunities for individual conversations were limited. But tonight, Linda arrived late and sat in the seat next to me. During the session, I studied her and her family without being too obvious. Her daughter was a couple of years older than my daughter and was always smiling with her parents. She seemed to have a great deal of respect and love for them, and a definite preference for her father. Linda's husband was reserved, but funny in an awkward way. He provided much-needed comic relief in these sessions. Linda and her husband were successful and smart, but they were completely opposite. Linda always appeared to be on her own agenda, a little scattered, but in charge.

Tonight, her nails were each painted a different color. I kept staring at them. They looked a bit funny, but I was envious that she had the confidence to paint her nails in a ridiculous rainbow of colors at her age, without caring what others would think of her. I frequently wondered why their daughter was in the group. She appeared to be a typical teen, always cheerful and cooperative. She presented nothing like my daughter, who couldn't make eye contact, was deathly afraid of speaking, and rocked back and forth to comfort herself.

During our five-minute break, Linda turned to me and said, "I am scared to death of what is going to happen to my daughter."

"Why?" I asked. "She looks so happy."

Linda went on to explain that her daughter is entering her final year of high school. She said, "I don't think she will ever be able to live alone. I don't think she will ever hold down a job. She used to be just like your daughter. We've been doing this for years. She's made progress but not enough. We agreed to do this program for her. It is our last chance of saving her."

My heart sunk for her. Tears filled her eyes and mine. I felt a lump form in my throat. I told Linda I felt like I was running out of time with my daughter. She assured me I had plenty of time left. We shared stories. We offered hope. We shared our greatest fears. But, most importantly we left that night feeling understood for the first time in our journeys, parenting children with severe mental illness.

Ending Stigma Begins with You

When we finally got confirmation that my daughter's issues were due to mental illness, I immediately told her that there was nothing to be ashamed of and no reason to hide. I shared with her my personal story of mental illness, which comforted her. She was relieved to know that she wasn't "bad" and what happened to her wasn't her fault. Once she learned of her diagnoses, she started to share with teachers, classmates, and friends. She was an open book. Sometimes, her honesty caused her to lose friends. Parents labeled her as a "bad" kid and the type that they didn't want their own kids to be around. She lost friends. Her siblings lost friends. I lost friends. It was painful, but we realized that those people were never really our friends. They turned their backs and walked away from us in our greatest time of need. Friends don't do that.

We were also judged. I was judged. My parenting was judged. People always thought they had the solutions. They could "turn my daughter" around. They could "shape her up." I learned to listen to these people, as they only meant well. They lacked the understanding of the severity of my daughter's mental illnesses. This wasn't a snap your fingers, give your daughter structure, she needs more rules, and then she will be "cured" journey. This was far from that. The top doctors in the state declared her one of the most challenging children they have worked with. Those words allowed me to breathe a sigh of relief and allow myself to stop judging myself as a mother. I was doing the best I could, given the circumstances, and so was my daughter.

Turn your eyes inward and look at ways you may be perpetuating the stigma of mental health. Are you hiding your child's mental illness, or are you asking your child to hide it? Are you ashamed or embarrassed? Are you not seeking outside support because of your own stigma of mental health? Think about how your actions and words are impacting your child, and what can you do differently going forward? Make notes in your journal and a plan for how you can change for the better!

First Steps to Building Your Tribe

As soon as I realized that I was doing the best I could as a mother, I took the first steps in building my tribe. I have spent the majority of my life being very private. It's just who I am. I always believed sharing my insecurities and fears were a sign of weakness. I also always assumed people didn't want to hear my story. Why would they? They have their own stories. But, after hearing Linda's story, I realized how important it was to share my story. Her story made me feel understood for the first time in my life. It gave me hope. It gave me the confidence to make myself vulnerable. So, I decided to reach out to like-minded people and share my story. As my social circle grew, I was accepting people who were invested in my emotional well-being, and in return, I was also invested in theirs.

We all know the impact friendships have on emotional health. Friendships increase personal happiness and lessen stress, improve self-confidence, and help people cope with loss or illness. True friends are there to support, not judge, offer hugs, not criticism, to listen with full attention, and love unconditionally. True friends will be there for you to lift you up when you say, "I can't" and will give you energy when you are feeling depleted. I have a handful of these friends and without them, my journey with my daughter's mental illness would have been a whole lot rockier.

And then there are what I call "Angel on Earth" friends. This is that one friend, who is not only a "Soul Sister," but the one person who you can call at 4:00 a.m. and they would jump in the car and drive hours to be by your side. That one person who would do everything and anything for you, and you would do the same for them. My Angel on Earth friend just happens to share my first name, Tanya. She was brought into my life months before my daughter was born. We frequently joke about becoming old ladies together, sitting on the beach reminiscing about the "good old days," the days when her son and my daughter were in middle school, and we didn't think we would survive.

Being a mom to a teen is no joke, but being a mom to a teen with emotional issues is really no joke. It takes a tribe to lift you up, encourage you to take the next step, tell you that you are a good mother and not a failure, and remind you that your daughter will be "OK," whatever "OK" means.

My Angel on Earth friend never says the wrong thing and never makes me feel bad about myself. She is the first person to say good morning to me via text and the last to say goodnight via text. When she doesn't know what to say, she tells me just that, and lets me know that she is with me and will never let me walk this journey alone. She is the one friend who understands the depth of my pain in raising a daughter with mental illness. She is truly an angel on Earth.

When building your sisterhood or tribe, you'll want to include true friends, an Angel on Earth friend, family, and other parents who are parenting a child with a mental illness. There are so many online support groups through social media or national organizations. Search these groups and join one or two. See if you can make some connections to start building your tribe. Additionally, you can ask your therapist, your child's doctors, or local hospitals for names of local support groups you can join. Connecting with other parents who are on this same journey can be life changing for you. If you are feeling isolated in raising your child with mental illness, I encourage you to step out of your comfort zone and find people who are walking your same journey. As you build your tribe, you'll be sharing your family's journey with mental illness. Sharing your story will increase awareness and help end the stigma associated with mental illness.

Part of your tribe will be your child's treatment team. One of the most exhausting parts of my journey was creating my daughter's treatment team. I would build one, we'd have months of appointments, and then discover one of the providers was slowing things down rather than moving things forward. Be patient. Progress can be incredibly slow. Follow your mama gut, as you know your child better than anyone.

If you are not seeing any progress after months, you may want to have an honest discussion with the provider and start looking for someone new. Build the strongest treatment team you can. You'll know when you are on the right path. In addition to her treatment team, you will have your own treatment team. Finding a supportive and skilled therapist can help you stay on the right path and keep your emotional health in balance.

My tribe knows that there are days that I will say, "I can't do this," but I always follow up with, "but, I can do it. I am doing it."

CHAPTER 11

STEP 8—SHINE ON MAMA BEAR! YOU ARE ROCKING THIS ROLE!

. . . .

"You did the best that you knew how. Now that you know better, You'll do better."

– Maya Angelou

My Journal Entry—Mother's Day 2019

Mother's Day has always been overrated in my book. I actually hate it. When you have a child with mental illness who has unpredictable moods, it's virtually impossible to schedule outings. Today, I texted my BFF and reminded her how much I dread this day and how I wish tomorrow would be here. This year, I will have no expectations, no plans, and will think of it as just another day. Honestly, every day should be Mother's Day, with the load mothers carry day in and out. Today, I feel free. It's nice not having expectations for the day, only to be disappointed later. Liv didn't acknowledge Mother's Day until bedtime. My heart ached for her, as she spent the day in her room angry. I could sense she wanted to reach out to me, but she just couldn't manage. Her mood was off. By bedtime, she was able to whisper, "Happy Mother's Day" and offer me a hug, which was a gift. Today, I spent the day celebrating myself and the warrior I have become. I journaled, meditated, gave myself Reiki, and just breathed. It was the perfect day celebrating myself and the gift of motherhood! I am grateful for this day!

Freedom

Letting go and accepting your child and their mood disorder is liberating. Once I was able to take this step, my life took a turn away from the darkness and back into the light. I realized my role as my daughter's mother was not to "fix" her of her mood disorder but to accept her and love her just as she was born to be.

It took me time to realize that I could be a better mom by accepting her for who she is, rather than who I wanted her to be. I was able to accept her illness. Once I did that, I was able to refocus my energy and provide her the love and support she needed to learn skills and make progress towards a life worth living. I knew that I would finally be a better mom because I knew better now. This freedom allowed me to move on to be the mom I always imagined I would be. I had more time to focus on myself, as I was spending less time trying to "fix" her.

As moms, we are expected to be master multitaskers, jacks of all trades, caregivers, wives, chefs, drivers, teachers, therapists, doctors, and as if that wasn't enough, career women, as many moms hold down part-time or full-time jobs. We are nurturers. We wipe tears, fix scraped knees, and give our families 110 percent of our time. When I realized that I could do better by giving less time, I also became a better mom. Motherhood has sucked the life out of me on many occasions. Sound familiar? I got to the point where I knew I needed to regain control of my life and happiness. I was trying too hard to help my daughter live her life up to my standards. My hopes and dreams for her were not the hopes and dreams she had for herself. She had, and still has, some unhealthy hopes and dreams. As her mother, it is my job to get her the support she needs to gain self-confidence and master skills so she can get back on track and learn how to cope and function in a much healthier way.

Rediscovering Yourself

Rediscovering yourself might feel intimidating at first. Perhaps you've been a mother for fifteen years, like me, and have given your life to your family. As women, we often view our role as mother, caregiver, and wife to mean no time for ourselves, with the exception of a girls' night out once a month or so. That's not enough. As women, we need to allow ourselves to rediscover our talents and interests. Or maybe you are like me, and you are ready to discover new interests. Excellent!

Scheduling time for yourself is a must. Put times and dates into your calendar. Don't schedule other appointments during this time unless it is absolutely necessary. Each week, I have appointments that I schedule in advance to take care of myself: the gym, acupuncture, Reiki, and therapy. These are my "must have" appointments as they make me feel physically and emotionally happier. What makes you feel physically and emotionally happier? Make a list. Grab your journal. Prioritize these and put them in your schedule.

Think about your physical health. What gives you energy and makes you feel physically healthier? Maybe walks, running, yoga, Pilates, or the gym? Make a list and schedule your favorite physical activities into your calendar at least three times a week for an hour, or split them into thirty-minute sessions.

Next, let's consider your emotional health. What are activities you can do to improve your emotional well-being? I have a weekly one-on-one session with my therapist. I also schedule time for daily meditation. I have my favorite apps on my phone and can meditate in the car when I have time throughout my day. If I arrive early to an appointment, I wait in my car and meditate.

As you know, I am a huge believer in affirmations, so I will share my favorite place online for affirmations! I discovered Louise Hay, who is known as one of the founders of the self-help movement. I follow @Louise_hay_affirmations on Instagram and have a collection of her books. Her website, louisehay.com, is a great resource. Her audiobooks, books, and daily affirmations have helped improve my mental well-being. I start my day with an affirmation and I repeat the affirmation throughout the day. My mind and mood is boosted when I incorporate positive affirmations into my daily routines.

In the previous chapter, we talked about building a tribe or sisterhood. Building time in your day to call, email, text, or spend time with a friend is critical for your emotional well-being. I often push people away in times of distress, but I have learned that reaching out always allows for more positive outcomes. My friends and family find satisfaction in helping me and I feel comforted by their love and support. I cherish the times I meet my friends for coffee or a lunch/dinner date. Let's face it, women are busy, but carving that time out to make the connection of being in each other's presence is therapeutic for the mind and heart.

Journaling

By now you also know that I love journaling. I have given you suggestions about what to journal, but here I want to explain an added benefit of journaling. One of my favorite things to do is to look back at last year's journal entries. Looking back and seeing how far we have come brings hope. I love seeing the growth in my parenting, the growth in my children, and the growth in my emotional and physical well-being. This transformation is captured throughout my journaling. Writing is therapeutic. If you don't have time for weekly therapy, put a journal in your purse and carry it with you throughout the day. I guarantee you will find time to journal when you are waiting at an appointment or waiting for your kids to get out of school at pickup time.

Goals

I have always had plenty of goals for my three daughters but realized I lost myself during the process of raising them. The goals I once had for myself were no longer my goals. When I was in third grade, I remember telling my friends that I was going to write children's book. I haven't achieved that goal quite yet, but I made a new goal to write a book for mothers about raising children with mood disorders.

When we have our own goals as mothers, it takes the pressure off our children. We learn to take our lives back and let them have more control over their lives. When we have goals, we will become happier and mentally healthier. Our confidence will grow, our self-worth will increase, and our lives will change for the better. I encourage my children to journal their goals and track their progress. I do the same. I will also encourage you to take out your journal and answer these questions. What goals do you have for yourself? How can you attain these goals? What is the first step you need to take to attain your goals? What help do you need to take the first step? The next step?

Exploring New Interests

When I began to explore new interests, I started exploring alternative practices for healing my mind and body. I already shared that I discovered Reiki (the healing energy of the universe), a hands-on healing system, when I was in the hospital recovering from a mastectomy. Reiki is used to promote healing, aide in deep relaxation, and reduce pain. It can help overcome the stress of parenting, relationships, and careers. It has also helped me release stuck emotional patterns. Through Reiki, I have expanded my consciousness and tapped into my internal creativity and wisdom. I went on to become a Reiki one and two practitioner. Not only did I love the practice of Reiki and the benefits it provided me and my children, but I also enjoyed spending time with people who shared common interests. It was refreshing discovering something I enjoyed that did not involve my children. The time away from home, to learn Reiki in a two-day workshop was rejuvenating in itself. It was time I needed to get myself centered.

One of my favorite ways to discover new interests and meet new people is through the app called Meetup or the Meetup website, www.meetup.com. Meetup is a site that brings people together to share common interests. There are Meetups for just about everything you can imagine: hiking, running, dating, learning to cook, practicing a language, meditation, mindfulness, anxiety, ADHD, personal growth, parenting, and so much more. This will require you to get out of your comfort zone and do something you might not typically do. You will meet new people who share similar interests and you just might discover that you have some hidden talents.

Once you are back on track and taking care of your mind and body, your moods will improve, your energy will increase, and the time you spend with your children will be quality time. You will have more patience and energy to deal with the tough days. You will look at your child in a whole new way. You'll let go of the judgment and embrace your child for who he or she was born to be.

CHAPTER 12

THE JOURNEY IS NEVER OVER

. . . .

"You don't have to have it all figured out to move forward … just take the next step."

– Unknown

My Journal Entry—August 24, 2019

It's 1:00 a.m., and I can't sleep. I can't wait to see Liv tomorrow. My heart still aches not having her home, but "I'm OK," because I know deep down inside she is getting the help and support she needs at her new residential school. I am also OK because I know my journey as Liv's mom is filled with hope. Life is a crazy ride and so is parenting. As I reflect back on my fifteen years of being a mom, I can't help but smile. I am proud of my daughters and proud of myself. We have overcome obstacles and heartache. I think about how lucky I am to have three girls who call me mom. We still have difficult days, but we rise to the challenges, and we do the best we know how at the time. It's not always perfect, and we make plenty of mistakes along the way, but we are gentle and kind to ourselves. We breathe. We accept. We grieve. We embrace the good and the bad, knowing day after day, we will keep putting one foot in front of another through the tears, anger, smiles, laughter, hate, and love. In eleven hours I'll see my girl again. I'm hoping the visit begins with a hug, but if it doesn't, I know I'll be OK.

A New Beginning

We have come to the end, but it is just the beginning and a chance for you to take that next step. You most certainly don't have it all figured out, but I know you have the courage to take that next step, because you have come this far. I have guided you through the WELLNESS process and its eight steps to handle your child's mood disorder without feeling like you are failing as a mother. As a mother, coach, teacher, and energy healer, I wrote this book to show other moms who are raising a child with a mood disorder that there is another way. Things can get better, despite the fact your child's mental illness will most likely be a lifelong battle.

As you know, children who have mood disorders are unpredictable and can have severe swings in their moods. If you are like me, you have fallen to your knees, thrown up your arms, and pleaded for an answer or maybe even begged for your child to be "cured." Like me, you have not found a cure or answer, but you now have the survival guide that has helped me and many others become healthier and happier parents on the journey of raising a child with a mood disorder. I keep my copy handy every day, so I am ready for whatever comes my way. My daughter's mood disorder still causes me and her pain, tears, uncertainty, and sadness, but I am better equipped at handling it and accepting it.

If you have tried finding help from doctors and therapists, and you are left feeling overwhelmed, worried, and responsible for your child's mental illness, do not allow these obstacles to make you give up. You are not failing as a parent. Through my research and work as a mental health coach and mother, as well as raising a child with a mood disorder, I have found a way to help. I now feel less frightened, less exhausted, and less lonely. There is hope. I have learned how to let in the light, even when the day is filled with darkness.

As you know, your child is watching you. They are looking at you for strength, acceptance, and love. They look at you to give them hope when they feel hopeless or strength when they feel weak. They live with this every minute of every day, and they will for the rest of their lives.

The WELLNESS process is a process that works and will provide you and your child with the hope you so desperately need. This process was created when I felt like I was failing as a mom. I honestly thought my children would be better off without me. You too can overcome the obstacles of raising a child with a mood disorder. Your child is depending on you. The WELLNESS process can lead you and your child to a healthier, happier, and more fulfilling life. You both have too much to offer this world and we need you to shine your light as bright as you can. Be a voice to stop the stigma of mental illness. Join me and so many others as we stand united to offer hope and healing to those affected by mental illness. Together we can make a difference.

As with most things in life, the WELLNESS process takes time and patience. It is not easy, but not changing the way you are handling your child's illness is not easy either. By picking up this book, you are already telling me your current way is not working. Your child deserves the best version of you, and so do you. If you are living your life day in and out through your child, you are not living. You are existing. You are barely breathing. I know because I have been there. There is a whole life out there waiting for you. There is a whole life out there waiting for your child.

You learned the steps that can help you reclaim your emotional health and your life. You will begin to discover joy, pride, and unconditional love for your child. When your child starts seeing you live joyfully with love and acceptance, they too will open their hearts and let the light shine through. Remember, you are not alone and never will be again.

ACKNOWLEDGMENTS

· ·

Writing this book was more rewarding than I imagined and would not have been possible without the blessings and encouragement of my daughters. Olivia, Ella, and Sienna, thank you for allowing me to share our story and for showing me the gifts that can come with mental illness: resilience, creativity, humor, empathy, and love. You will undoubtedly use these gifts to change the world! During our family's journey with mental illness, when days were very dark, I began to believe that something positive would come out of the heartache mental illness was causing our family. I prayed, meditated, listened, and watched for signs. Eventually, one after another, stars aligned, and my soul's purpose was revealed; writing this book and sharing the message of hope and healing with families like ours; families who know the pain and sadness mental illness can cause. Remember, when life throws you a curve ball, believe in yourself and look for the goodness in the situation. Your strength and courage will carry you far in life! Dream big, stay true to yourself, and follow your heart! I love you!

To my Angel on Earth, Tanya Ferretto: thank you, soul sister, for believing in me when I didn't believe in myself, for lifting me up when I had no strength, for listening, caring, laughing, crying, and supporting me through this crazy ride called motherhood! This book would not be possible without you cheering me on and encouraging me to take the leap. I will forever remember the first day we met as new neighbors, with big bellies and even bigger smiles, awaiting the arrival of our babies. You exuded happiness and kindness, and still do. You also have a remarkable way with words, always knowing just what I need to hear. I can't wait until we are in our eighties, relaxing on the beach (yes, the beach!), reminiscing about our long days raising toddlers and teens! We will still remind each other to breathe, but it will have a whole new meaning! I love and cherish you!

I want to thank my parents for teaching me at a very young age that the impossible is possible. To BKT, my angel mom, thank you for showing me signs that you are on this journey with me. Thank you for raising me to be a strong, independent woman who is capable of achieving greatness, when I allow myself to believe. To my dad, KPT, for opening your heart and having the courage to marry my mom, a single mom with three young kids, and for taking on the role as our dad. By far, you have been one of the greatest gifts in my life. My early days of writing were with you and Edward R. Murrow. You taught me to challenge myself beyond measure and never choose the easier path. To Bev, for opening your heart and extending your love, kindness, and support to our family. Thank you for sharing your love of books and adventure with us!

To my siblings, for supporting me, loving me, and always pushing me to go big. To Kim, for being my go-to person to bounce ideas off when writing this book, and for the tireless and important work you do with teens who have mental health conditions. The love you have for your students shines through you. I love and admire you! Jen, thank you for always being my voice of reason. May today and every day be a double mocha day. I love you more than you love Starbucks! To my big brother, Denny, for teaching me how to use my voice with confidence and how to survive on little sleep! The best compliment I have ever received was when my third-grade teacher called me "Little Denny." To Stacey, who has shown me that illness does not define who we are but that the strength and character that we portray while fighting the illness does. I am in awe of your strength and courage and thank you for inspiring me and the girls.

My heartfelt thanks to Maria and Sophia, my soul sister and soul daughter, for your unconditional love, acceptance, and friendship. Thank you for showing us the meaning of authentic friendship through your selfless acts of kindness and honesty. For making us laugh when we needed to laugh and for offering us a shoulder when we needed to cry. Maria, thank you for raising your daughter to accept, love, and support people with mental illness. The world needs more of you! Sophie, you are wise beyond your years and will go on to change the world. I can't wait to read your book. Your heart, compassion, humor, intelligence, and intuition will allow you to succeed in whatever you set out to accomplish. Thank you both for your part in fighting to end the stigma of mental illness, and for opening your hearts to us. We love you!

To Shannon, for showing me the depth of pain that mental illness can cause and for showing me how to have the courage and strength to fight for hope and healing. You have inspired me to reach out and touch the lives of those living with mental illness. Thank you for your honesty and willingness to share your own story. I love you!

I want to express my gratitude to my co-parent for telling me you wanted a divorce in the midst of me writing this book, before my married name went on the cover! May our three girls overcome any obstacle that comes their way with strength, acceptance, love, and grace. Thank you for blessing me with them, the greatest gift.

To my friends (you know who you are), your support got me through some very challenging days. I am grateful for your love and blessed to call you my friends, my sisters. Thank you for being you!

To the Author Incubator Team, especially Angela Lauria, for creating a platform where people with servants' hearts can share messages of hope and healing through books. Thank you for having the confidence in my message and for giving me the opportunity to say, "YES"! For Emily, for pushing me beyond my comfort zone and for encouraging me to "keep writing forward." Thank you for your invaluable contributions and guiding me in the home stretch. For Cheyenne, a ray of CA sunshine, who skillfully took a daunting process and made it attainable. For the entire Author Incubator Team, thank you for the part you took in helping make my dream a reality! Finally, thank you to David Hancock and the Morgan James Publishing team for helping me bring this book to print.

A very special thanks to Melissa Boyd. This book would not have been possible without your spiritual guidance, coaching, and mentorship. I found you by chance while vacationing in Maine, and you changed my life forever! You have helped me unlock my true potential and reach for the stars. Your gift has blessed me and so many others. Namaste.

To our friends who turned their backs on us and walked away in our time of need. May you begin to see the gifts of those living with mental illness.

To my Liv, you make me burst with pride. Your voice and strength have helped change the stigma of mental health in your school and our community. I admire your willingness to share your story and also admire your courage to gently push away people who don't accept you. You will continue to use your resilience and voice to pave the way for other children with mental illness. Always let your light shine through. You are destined for greatness! I love you!

Finally, to children who are living with mental illness, and parents who are raising them, there is light even in the midst of the darkest days. You are loved, valued, and accepted just the way you are. May you find comfort knowing you are not alone.

THANK YOU!

· ·

Thank you for reading this book and for joining me on this journey. My wish is that you will have a renewed sense of hope as you to continue on your journey parenting a child with a mental health condition.

I am here to support you long after you put this book down. I encourage you to keep this book handy and use it as a daily survival guide. I would also love to connect and learn more about your journey, so please reach out.

As a way to say thank you, I have created a video series, *8 Steps to Handle Your Child's Mood Disorder without Feeling Like a Failure*. Each day, for eight days, you will receive a video from me by email. Sign up at www.tanyatrevett.com

I look forward to connecting and walking on this path toward hope and healing with you!

ABOUT THE AUTHOR

Tanya Trevett is a mental health coach, teacher, Reiki practitioner, and author of Help, I'm Failing as a Mom! Tanya coaches parents who have children with mental health conditions to navigate school, home, and our complex mental health system in a way that offers them hope. She is the mother of three daughters with mental health conditions and a devoted advocate fighting to end the stigma of mental illness in our country. She lives in Massachusetts.

REFERENCES

· ·

Cree RA, Bitsko RH, Robinson LR, Holbrook JR, Danielson ML, Smith DS, Kaminski JW, Kenney MK, Peacock G. Health care, family, and community factors associated with mental, behavioral, and developmental disorders and poverty among children aged 2–8 years—United States, 2016. MMWR, 2018;67(5):1377–1383.

https://www.cdc.gov/childrensmentalhealth/data.html#ref